BRUNO AND LEWIS

BRUNO AND LEWIS

THE BOXING YEARS

RALPH OATES

FONTHILL

Fonthill Media Language Policy

Fonthill Media publishes in the international English language market. One language edition is published worldwide. As there are minor differences in spelling and presentation, especially with regard to American English and British English, a policy is necessary to define which form of English to use. The Fonthill Policy is to use the form of English native to the author. Ralph Oates was born and educated in England; therefore British English has been adopted in this publication.

Fonthill Media Limited
Fonthill Media LLC
www.fonthillmedia.com
office@fonthillmedia.com

First published in the United Kingdom and the United States of America 2017

British Library Cataloguing in Publication Data:
A catalogue record for this book is available from the British Library

Copyright © Ralph Oates 2017

ISBN 978-1-78155-590-3

The right of Ralph Oates to be identified as the author of this work has been asserted by him in accordance with the Copyright, Designs and Patents Act 1988.

All rights reserved. No part of this publication may be reproduced, stored in a retrieval system or transmitted in any form or by any means, electronic, mechanical, photocopying, recording or otherwise, without prior permission in writing from Fonthill Media Limited

Typeset in 11pt on 13pt MinionPro
Printed and bound by CPI Group (UK) Ltd, Croydon, CR0 4YY

Foreword

During the nearly thirty years that I worked for the British Boxing Board of Control, I was fortunate and privileged enough to have met some of the greatest heavyweight champions of this and the last century, including Muhammad Ali; Joe Frazier; and the Klitschko brothers, Vitali and Wladimir. However it was not until 1993 that I could claim to have met and worked (in my capacity as an official) with a British world heavyweight champion. That was Lennox Lewis, closely followed in 1994 by Herbie Hide, and then a year later by the nation's favourite, Frank Bruno. Like London buses, you wait for ages and then three come along one after the other!

I had watched Big Frank win the ABA Heavyweight Championship on television in 1980, but there had already been a buzz about this exciting new heavyweight prospect from South London before that. When he finally had his first professional contest at the Royal Albert Hall two years later, I had no doubt on the night that, despite the championship fight topping the bill, a substantial section of the big crowd (particularly around the ringside area) had come to see Bruno's debut, He was someone who all boxing dreamers fervently hoped would end the eighty-five-year drought, stretching back to Bob Fitzsimmons in 1897, and deliver a British world heavyweight champion. It took a while, with some ups and downs along the way, but the lad got there!

Lewis had got there already two years earlier, in 1993. I met him first in 1989 while working ringside at a tournament also at the Royal Albert Hall. I was asked by Frank (now Kelly) Maloney if I would go with him up to one of the private boxes to meet the then current Olympic super-heavyweight Champion, along with some sponsors, as he wished to turn professional in the country of his birth with Maloney as his manager. I happily agreed, and that was my first encounter with the charming, intelligent young man with the soft Canadian accent who would go on to dominate the world heavyweight scene in the 1990s and early 2000s.

Throughout their careers, I had a fair bit of contact with both—mostly on the scales, at ringside, or in the dressing room, alongside the occasional boxing- or sport-related social function. I found both, in their different ways, to be friendly, courteous, and very professional. It was easy to develop a good working relationship with both, and I was honoured to have been invited to Frank's world championship victory celebrations in the West End. Sometime later, I was equally honoured to attend a reception at the House of Commons, hosted by three MPs from the Conservative, Labour, and Liberal Democrat parties, to honour Lewis's world title successes.

Lewis provided me with one of my most memorable nights ever when he defended his title against American Michael Grant in 2000 at Madison Square Garden—the most renowned venue in boxing. To take my ringside seat at such a venue in order to watch a British heavyweight champion of the world defend his title was, for a lifelong fan and failed novice amateur boxer like me, a dream come true—and one not granted to any of my illustrious predecessors as General Secretary.

The showdown between Lewis and Bruno came in 1993 in a contest that lived up to all the hype. A wet Cardiff Arms Park was the venue, but both men proved, in victory and defeat respectively, that they belonged in that elite ring.

If anyone is going to put together the story of how these two British boxing legends and their different paths eventually came together, then it is my friend, Ralph Oates. My bookshelf already contains a host of his books, and his knowledge of the history of our sport is unsurpassed. For those who were around in the '80s and '90s—or those who have just come to the sport—beg, steal, borrow (but preferably buy!) a copy of this book and remind yourself (or learn for the first time) how this clash of the titans came about, and how they both fared afterwards.

Simon Block
Hon. Secretary, Commonwealth Boxing Council
General Secretary, British Boxing Board of Control
2000–2008

My personal thanks to Howard Oates for his assistance in checking the information in the book. Dedicated to the memory of Ruby Oates, who was a very special lady.

I would also like to thank my good friend Simon Block for penning the foreword to the book. Photographs are courtesy of Les Clark, Derek Rowe and Philip Sharkey. Finally, many thanks to Jay Slater and John Vincent of Fonthill Media.

CONTENTS

Boxing Organisations

ABA:	Amateur Boxing Association
EBU:	European Boxing Union
IBC:	International Boxing Council
IBF:	International Boxing Federation
IBU:	International Boxing Union
NABF:	North American Boxing Federation
NBA:	National Boxing Association
NYSAC:	New York State Athletic Commission
OPBF:	Oriental and Pacific Boxing Federation
PABA:	Pan American Boxing Association
USBA:	United States Boxing Association
WBA:	World Boxing Association
WBC:	World Boxing Council
WBO:	World Boxing Organisation

Introduction

I think we would all agree, without fear of contradiction, that the heavyweight division is the flagship in boxing, for it is the weight division that appeals to the masses. To become the heavyweight champion of the world is the ultimate prize in the square ring—it really is something special. Fighters who have won this crown are in great demand; their services sought-after both inside the ring and outside of said battleground. Their names are often known above many other personalities in the sporting world.

To become the heavyweight champion of the world is the dream for any contender. The road to the championship can be both long and hard, but, if achieved, the fighter concerned can be assured of fame beyond his wildest dreams. Those golden words, 'the heavyweight champion of the world', are a sentence that demands attention and respect.

These days, of course, the situation is a little complicated, due to there being four major boxing organisations (the WBC, WBA, IBF, and WBO), which means it is possible to have four world heavyweight champions reigning at the same time—perhaps even more when some of the lesser regarded organisations in operation are factored in. This somewhat dilutes the value of the title to some degree, but in truth any one of the major versions of the championship is realistically still worth winning.

This four-way championship is, of course, a problem that affects all divisions in the sport. This is a situation which does not sit well with the purists of boxing, who feel there should be one world champion in every weight division, a view which is difficult to argue with. It goes without saying that it really would be ideal to have just one man who is king of his respected division. Thankfully, the rival champions meet in unification contests from time to time to see who the better man at the weight really is—the winner becoming the undisputed champion, even if only for a short time. I say 'for a short time' because it is often difficult for the undisputed title holder to meet their mandatory challengers and to accommodate the demands from all the various organisations—and therein lies the problem, since this can lead to at least one of the versions of the title being stripped from the champion should he be unable to adhere to said edict. This is far from an ideal situation, since it once again splits the titles—a backward step for boxing, with the championship again being shared between different fighters. I cannot help but feel this is a problem that could easily be avoided if only common sense was applied.

In previous years, the USA had a firm grip on the division, with it having been split, or otherwise. Men like Bob Fitzsimmons (England), Tommy Burns (Canada), Max Schmeling (Germany), Primo Carnera (Italy), Ingemar Johansson (Sweden), and Trevor Berbick (Canada) were the very few who had been able to break the stranglehold and tear the championship away from American hands.

The reign of the few who were able to win the championship did not last too long, with the exception of Burns, who held the crown from 1906–1908. Despite the difficult task of being able to defeat an American heavyweight champion, many challengers from various countries put their hopefuls forward only to see them repelled by the often superior American title holder. Great Britain also pitted its best heavyweights into the ring to contest the championship, only to find that the title was way beyond their reach and failure the depressing end result.

The USA turned out a number of great fighters—indeed, outstanding fighters—at heavyweight, men like Jack Johnson, Jack Dempsey, Rocky Marciano, Floyd Patterson, Muhammad Ali, Joe Frazier, George Foreman, Larry Holmes—the list seems endless. The USA owned the division. The championship was theirs—the only competition had come from within their own country. Whenever a British fighter stepped up to challenge for the championship, he was not taken seriously in the USA. Even domestic fans knew that, unless he got lucky or the title holder had a bad night, he was not going to win. Fans wondered why the UK could not produce a Louis, a Marciano, or, dare I say, an Ali.

Then, after many years of disappointment, a ray of hope finally shone for the UK, when Frank Bruno emerged, followed later by Lennox Lewis. These two boxers appeared to be the answer to Britain's hopes for a heavyweight world crown. They both seemed to have the necessary skills to end the American dominance and put the UK on the map as a serious threat to the heavyweight crown.

While this book concentrates on the efforts of Bruno and Lewis, it is not forgotten that both Henry Akinwande and Herbie Hide also played their part in building the reputation of British heavyweights globally during that time, by winning versions of the world title.

This book does not impinge on the personal lives of Bruno and Lewis; it concentrates only on their activities in the ring and on the boxing front, and their ultimate climb to the top. It takes a look at the exciting ride they both took and the opponents they fought along the way, as well as the difficulties they overcame on their ascendancy towards winning the world heavyweight championship—including their eventual clash inside the ring.

I do hope you enjoy the book and find it adds to the many happy, unforgettable moments they gave the fans with their respective endeavours.

Ralph Oates
Norfolk
October 2016

1

Frank Bruno

When Frank Bruno made his foray into professional boxing, much was expected of this exciting young fighter. Britain had waited anxiously for many years for a boxer who would bring the world heavyweight title back to the UK.

At the time, the only world heavyweight champion Britain could lay claim to was Bob Fitzsimmons, who held the crown from 1897–1899. Charlie Mitchell was the first Briton to have a crack at the title under the Marquess of Queensberry rules prior to the success of Fitzsimmons. Later, Gunner Moir, Jack Palmer, Jem Roche, Jewey Smith, Tommy Farr, Bruce Woodcock, Don Cockell, Brian London (twice), Henry Cooper, Joe Bugner, and Richard Dunn all duly climbed into the ring to contest the championship, only to come away empty-handed. Such was the extent of the dismal failure of our heavyweights on the world stage that they were unflatteringly dubbed the 'Horizontal Heavyweights'.

Bruno, at a height of 6 feet 3 inches, ticked all the boxes and looked to have the tools to climb the lofty championship ladder and hence change the less than respectful views the boxing world held about the world-class pretentions of British heavyweights in general. To his credit, Bruno was a puncher who could put the lights out of his opponent once he connected, and this has always been an advantage in boxing.

During his time in the amateur ranks, Frank won the ABA heavyweight title, outpointing Welshman Rudi Pika over three rounds in a contest that took place in 1980. In doing so at the age of eighteen, Bruno became the youngest man in the division to win this championship, and a career in the paid ranks beckoned.

Bruno was born on 16 November 1961 in Hammersmith, London. He turned professional under manager Terry Lawless—a man who had taken a number of fighters to British, Commonwealth, and European titles in various weight divisions. His roster included three world champions in the shape of John H. Stracey (WBC welterweight), Maurice Hope (WBC super-welterweight—poundage then called light-middleweight), and Jim Watt (WBC lightweight). In fact, it could be said that Lawless was to boxing what Brian Epstein was to pop music. Epstein had famously discovered the likes of The Beatles, Cilla Black, Billy J. Kramer and the Dakotas, Gerry and the Pacemakers, etc. Both Lawless and Epstein had a knack for developing the skills and talents of their respective charges to their full potential. While it was clear that Lawless could be proud of his many champions, it would be his ultimate success and the grandest feather in his cap if he could produce what British boxing was craving so badly for: a world heavyweight champion.

Due to constant disappointment through the years, many fans had given up hope of ever seeing a British fighter in their lifetime winning this title. Many hopefuls had emerged—good, talented fighters—but they were never able to compete with our American cousins, who always had the upper hand and turned back the UK challengers. The question was whether Frank Bruno really was the man to answer the dreams of the nation? Or would he be just another forlorn hope, a false alarm, who would be blown away like a leaf in a strong wind when faced with class opposition? Only time would tell.

However, before Bruno could punch for pay, he had to overcome a difficulty outside the ring that threatened his professional career before it had even started. Bruno had a rare form of short-sightedness that required him to travel to South America to undergo an operation to correct it. There were very few doctors at the time who had the required knowledge and capability to rectify said problem. Terry Lawless investigated the matter fully and was advised by a specialist that there were only two medical facilities in the world who would be able to carry out this kind of delicate operation. One was in Moscow, Russia, the other in Bogotá, Colombia. The Bruno team opted for the one in Bogotá—not exactly a bus ride down the road, but a necessary trip nevertheless.

Bruno packed his suitcase to make the journey in the hope that said operation would resolve the problem and save his boxing career. It was obviously a time of great concern for the fighter, but it proved to be a tale of triumph over adversity. The procedure, carried out by Spanish-born José Ignacio Barraquer, proved successful. Bruno later passed the stringent eye test and was duly licensed by the British Boxing Board of Control to start his boxing career. It could be said that Bruno had won his first major fight without even entering the ring or, indeed, throwing a punch. It was now all systems go.

Lupe Guerra

Bruno made his much-anticipated first appearance in the professional ranks at the Royal Albert Hall in London on 17 March 1982, against Mexican-born Lupe Guerra. While Mexico had a tradition of producing good fighters in the lower-weight divisions, even great ones, the nation was not renowned for world-class heavyweights. Only one Mexican at that time had challenged for a version of the world heavyweight title: Manuel Ramos. On 24 June 1968, Ramos had entered the ring at Madison Square Garden, New York, in an attempt to wrest the New York State Athletic Commission heavyweight crown from its formidable holder, Joe Frazier. He was stopped by Frazier in the second round.

That said, Guerra was not a bad test for the British boxer's debut. Guerra had fought twenty-three times, winning seventeen and losing six of his bouts, so he was by no means a pushover. The professional debut of a fighter, especially one who has been hyped, can be a nerve-racking experience for those backing him—let alone the fighter himself, who is expected to perform. The public's expectation of a win puts extra pressure on the night's young hopeful.

Once Bruno took off his robe before the contest started, it was clear to the many spectators in attendance that his fitness could certainly not be faulted. His chiselled physique would surely have made even Hercules jealous.

Guerra heard the bell to start the first round, but he did not hear the bell to start the second. Bruno found the punches to knock out his opponent in the opening session of an eight-round contest. Bruno carried out his task without working up a sweat and looked tremendous in doing so, scoring two knockdowns before landing the pay-off punch to end the bout. It was a dream debut for Bruno in the paid ranks. The first hurdle was over, but it was early days, and there would be sterner tests along the heavyweight path. The fast victory gave the fans hope that this could just be the man who might go all the way to the top. One thing was for certain: in Bruno, the promoters had a marketable fighter who would attract attention and, in turn, fill seats.

Coincidentally, Bruno's debut was on the anniversary of former world heavyweight champion Rocky Marciano's debut in 1947, when he had knocked out his opponent, Lee Epperson, in round three. Marciano went on to become a heavyweight great, retiring from the game with an undefeated record from forty-nine fights. Some may have wondered if this was an omen, however, no one truly expected Bruno to emulate the American's achievements—that really would be expecting too much. If he could accomplish just 50 per cent, or even 30 per cent, of what Rocky had achieved during his career, there would most certainly be no complaints from the fans.

Harvey Steichen

American Harvey Steichen was the next to test Bruno on 30 March 1982 at Wembley Arena. Steichen's record was one that was not going to keep Bruno or his management team up at night tearing their hair out with great concern. Having lost thirteen of his thirty-two bouts, Steichen's CV did not make for frightening reading. There were two standout names on his slate though: one was John Tate, the former WBA world heavyweight king, who had outpointed him over ten rounds on 15 February 1981. The other was future IBF heavyweight champion Tony Tucker, who stopped him in the third round in a contest later the same year (16 September).

At first sight, it could be said (with a degree of justification) that Steichen was a slight step down for Bruno after his debut contest against Lupe Guerra. However, to his credit, Steichen did manage to last a little longer than the Mexican. In a bout scheduled for eight rounds, he was stopped in its second stanza. Bruno carried out the task with ruthless efficiency, finding his way through his opponent's defence to land his explosive punches, which boded well for Bruno's future at that stage of his career.

On the same card, Bruno's former amateur opponent, Rudi Pika, notched up his seventh consecutive victory by outpointing Steve Gee over eight rounds. Pika, like Bruno, looked to be a fighter with promise. Pika had given Bruno a tough fight when they had met in the ABA final and a future bout between the pair looked a distinct possibility should they both keep on winning. Sadly, such a contest did not come to fruition, as Pika sadly took his own life on 26 May 1988.

Abdul Muhaymin

Bruno was soon back in the ring. The venue this time was the Royal Albert Hall in Kensington, London, on 20 April 1982, to face another American in a contest scheduled for eight rounds. The fighter squaring up in the opposite corner was Abdul Muhaymin (then named Tom Stevenson). Muhaymin was not able to stand up to Bruno's concussive punching and was unceremoniously knocked out in the first round. This proved to be an easy night for the British boxer, and some might be forgiven for thinking that Bruno was up against a soft touch. However, such thoughts were incorrect since Muhaymin had come to the UK with a decent record consisting of eleven victories and one defeat. The lone set-back had been a five-round stoppage loss due to cuts over the eyes against James Douglas on 14 October

1981—the very same Douglas who would go on and produce a massive shock in the years to come by knocking out an undefeated Mike Tyson for the world heavyweight championship in round ten on 11 February 1990. With that one fact alone, it has to be said that this was a good win by Bruno at this early stage of his career against a man who, at the time, had his own ambitions in the sport, and was thus not a constant loser who had come to the UK just to pick up his pay cheque and go home.

Ronald Gibbs

Bruno punched his way to another victory on 4 May 1982, this time over American Ronald Gibbs at Wembley Arena. Gibbs, at the time of the fight, did not have the kind of record that would put trepidation into his opponent's mind with it standing at 5 wins and 2 defeats. No one really thought for one minute that Gibbs was going to be a road block in Bruno's career, or indeed travel the full eight rounds. At this early stage of his career, Bruno's advisors were not going to put him in with anyone dangerous, as it would have been foolhardy to do so. The victory looked a mere formality for Bruno, and so it proved when he hammered his man to score the expected win. Nevertheless, Gibbs did manage to take Bruno into the fourth round, the furthest he had been to date, before the referee stepped in to stop the contest in the home fighter's favour. At the very least, Gibbs should be given credit for taking Bruno the extra rounds before the way to the exit door was shown to him.

Tony Moore

In his fifth contest, which took place on 1 June 1982 at the Royal Albert Hall in Kensington, Bruno met London-based Tony Moore. Moore was an opponent who did not look likely to give Bruno any serious difficulties. However, Bruno was meeting a fighter who looked capable of at least pushing him a few rounds, thus testing his stamina to see if he was able to cope should the fight drag on into the later stages. To that end, this looked a meaningful and sensible match, a good yardstick with which to measure Bruno's progress in the punch-for-pay ranks at the time.

Moore, during a long career that started on 10 June 1974 with a six-round points win over John Depledge, had comprised a record of fifty-five fights, winning twenty-two, losing twenty-five, and drawing eight. While Moore had lost more than he had won, he still had to be respected, as he had paid his dues in the professional ring and knew how to handle himself. In fact, Moore's record made interesting reading, as there were a few notable names on his CV, including future British heavyweight champion Neville Meade, who he met on three occasions.

The first bout against Meade took place on 29 April 1975, with Moore winning when his opponent retired in round five. The second meeting between the two occurred on 5 June 1975, the contest being declared a draw over eight rounds. The third in their trilogy of bouts saw Meade get revenge over Moore on 24 September 1975, winning on points over eight rounds. Then, on 30 November 1976, Moore went against the script, when he did the unexpected and defeated the former British and Commonwealth heavyweight king Danny McAlinden, who retired in four rounds. Moore had a return with Danny McAlinden on 14 December 1980, which resulted in another win for him—this time by way of an eight-round points victory.

Another name that more than stood out on Moore's record was Trevor Berbick, who had stopped him in round six in their bout, which took place on 1 August 1978 in Nova Scotia, Canada. While that was a clear defeat, it was by no means a disgrace coming second to Berbick, or, indeed being halted by this fighter, since it should be remembered that the Jamaican-born Canadian was a hot prospect on the way up, who would later exchange punches with a number of top-named fighters in his career. Berbick went on to challenge Larry Holmes for the WBC heavyweight crown in Las Vegas on 11 April 1981, losing a fifteen-round points decision. He later defeated the great, three-time world heavyweight king Muhammad Ali on points over ten rounds on 11 December 1981 in the Bahamas (albeit, Ali was now a much-faded fighter who was way past his best, being a mere shadow of the athlete he once was).

Berbick then made his mark and proved his worth by going against the general consensus of opinion and providing a shock by winning the WBC world heavyweight title on 22 March 1986, outpointing American holder, Pinklon Thomas, over twelve rounds in Las Vegas.

The scene was set for an interesting, and perhaps testing, night for Bruno, against a man who had shared the ring with good fighters and was not likely to be overawed or intimidated by the occasion. The ever-growing reputation of his young opponent would not trouble him in any way whatsoever. It was not on the cards that Moore would beat Bruno, but it was possible that he had enough know-how to fend him off with some old professional tricks of the trade, and hence last into the later stages of the fight. However, once again the contest, scheduled for the duration of eight rounds, concluded in two, with a victory for the undefeated fighter from the Lawless stable, who pulled off the win without suffering any form of inconvenience. It was obvious that Bruno packed real power in his punching, and that was always an asset in the ring.

George Scott

On 14 September 1982, Bruno stepped into the ring to take on Newcastle's George Scott, who was indulging in his twenty-second bout, having won eleven, lost seven, and drawn three. On his ledger, George had victories over future British heavyweight champion Gordon Ferris, who he stopped in three rounds on 7 February 1978, and an eight-round points decision win over former British and Commonwealth heavyweight king Danny McAlinden on 20 November 1979.

Scott was not going to add Bruno's name to his list of victims, and it would have been a surprise (indeed, something of a shock) had he lasted the full eight rounds. There were, indeed, no shocks of any kind during the bout; no staggering surprises to rock the sporting world at the Empire Pool, Wembley.

Bruno was not going to linger any longer than necessary in this encounter. He quickly took the action to his opponent and won his sixth bout with a stoppage in the first round, once again showing his power in no uncertain way. Scott was never in the fight, and was not able to put any kind of pressure on Bruno during the short time the fight lasted. Sometimes a fighter will protest should he feel that the referee acted prematurely in ending the fight—there were no complaints about the quick stoppage by Scott or, indeed, his corner.

Many boxers during their careers acquire a nickname, and at this time an appropriate one for Bruno might have been 'The Magician', since he was making his opponents disappear long before the final bell.

Bruno's speed of victories did not please everyone. Many critics were losing their patience somewhat. They felt that he was being protected and being fed opponents who had seen better days, who therefore lacked the necessary skill and ambition to make a real fight of it—that, in truth, the subsequent wins proved very little. To a degree, this point of view was understandable, but this was the nature of the sport. Young boxers have to be nurtured; brought along slowly; learn the game from fighters considered journeymen, the likes of who had been around for a number of years. They were decent enough opponents but not really likely to throw a spanner in the works. Former world champions like Joe Louis, Rocky Marciano, and George Foreman (plus many others) went down the same route at the start of their respective careers, winning a number of their early bouts well before the final round was reached.

World beaters are not developed overnight, in six minutes, or six fights. They have to hone their skills with a series of carefully planned learning fights, whereupon they can further their ring education. Then, when it is felt that the time is right, they are moved up a level.

Ali Lukasa

In his seventh bout, which took place in Germany, Bruno continued to show his punching prowess with a second-round stoppage of Ali Lukasa, who was born in Kinshasa, the Democratic Republic of the Congo. Lukasa entered the ring in Berlin on 23 October 1982 with a record of eighteen fights: thirteen victories and five defeats. That was not a bad CV, but Lukasa looked booked for defeat even before the bell sounded. Bruno was far too powerful for his opponent, who looked ready to fall as soon as Bruno found his target with his hurtful blows.

Two names of note who Lukasa had jousted with in the ring were former European champion Lucien Rodriguez, who stopped him in round four on 26 February 1981; and another former European title holder, Alfredo Evangelista, who knocked him out in round six on 29 April 1982, in the contest prior to Lukasa's meeting with Bruno. Based on those past outcomes, it was never likely that Lukasa would trouble, or indeed upset, the British fighter in a bout scheduled for eight rounds. This contest was a useful exercise for Bruno since it enabled him to fight in another country and hence get the feel of boxing outside his comfort zone.

Rudy Gauwe

The next fighter to face the heavy punches of Bruno in an eight-round bout was Rudy Gauwe from Belgium. Gauwe had a record of twenty-seven bouts, winning eighteen, losing seven, and drawing two. In truth, he appeared to have little chance of pulling off a win against his undefeated opponent.

Gauwe had, on 22 April 1980, contested the vacant European title with another fighter who had been with the Lawless stable, John L. Gardner; this resulted in a defeat when he retired in round nine of the contest, which took place at the Royal Albert Hall in London. Gauwe did not fare a great deal better in his second visit to the Royal Albert Hall in Kensington, on 9 November 1982. In fact, he fared a great deal worse. Bruno bettered his former stablemate's victory when he detonated his bombs, thus despatching his man in round two by way of a knockout.

While some pundits were still very critical of Bruno's opponents and baying for him to meet a better class of fighter, it had to be emphasised that he was still just a work in progress, and this was only his eighth paid outing. To his credit, Bruno was getting rid of this class of opponent the way he should. Had Gauwe been able to hold on until the later rounds, this would have been a point of concern.

George Butzbach

Germany's blond-haired George Butzbach was the next to fight the British hope at the Wembley Arena on 23 November 1982. In truth, Butzbach, the former German heavyweight champion, did not bring a great deal to the party on the night, being stopped inside the first round of a bout scheduled for eight. Butzbach was put on the deck within minutes of the opening stanza after taking a hard blow from Bruno. Butzbach took a count of seven from the referee but, on regaining his feet, held his hand up to signal that he had had enough for the night.

When viewing the result, one had to wonder whether it was worth the trip over to the UK for Butzbach. In fairness, Butzbach was not a bad choice of opponent for Bruno at this stage of his career—he came with a record of fifteen wins, three defeats, and three draws, and held a ten-round points victory over former European heavyweight champion Jean-Pierre Coopman in a contest that had taken place on 1 November 1979. Prior to fighting Bruno, Butzbach had lost only one fight inside the scheduled distance, and that was when he retired in round six against South African Kallie Knoetze on 14 September 1979. Bruno may not have added much to his ring know-how in this contest, but it confirmed that he was a genuine puncher and was clearly a level above this kind of opponent.

Three days later, in the USA, Larry Holmes made the thirteenth defence of his WBC world heavyweight crown in Houston on 26 November 1982, outpointing fellow American Randall 'Tex' Cobb over fifteen rounds in Houston. While Bruno was obviously a long way from this level of competition, there were high hopes that one day he would be involved in such marquee fights.

Gilberto Acuna

On 7 December 1982, the Royal Albert Hall saw Bruno in action once more before the year came to a close. The man in the opposite corner was Gilberto

Acuna from Costa Rica, a fighter who did not look capable of extending the British hope, let alone defeating him. Acuna's record was thirteen wins and eight defeats. He had previously fought in the UK twice before, with mixed success. On 11 October 1977, he was stopped in six rounds at the Seymour Hall in Marylebone, London, by the very capable Billy Aird. Then, on 13 October 1982, he knocked out Eddie Cooper in three rounds at the Assembly Hall in Walthamstow. An interesting name on Acuna's record was Joe Bugner, the former British, European, and Commonwealth heavyweight king, who put pay to Acuna at the Forum in Inglewood, California, stopping him in six rounds on 23 August 1980.

The Bruno-Acuna contest was scheduled for ten rounds, but it was painfully obvious the fight was not going to last that long. More painful, perhaps, for Acuna, was when Bruno gave him his ninth defeat by stopping him in the first round. Bruno improved his record to ten undefeated professional bouts all inside the distance, with five victories coming inside the first round.

The wins by Bruno were achieved without a great deal of effort and looked good on paper, but they were still a bone of contention with many critics, who were most anxious to see him face more demanding opposition. Terry Lawless clearly had plans for his young heavyweight hope and was determined that he was not going to be forced by public pressure to move his man up in class until he felt he was ready. Lawless was a man who knew the fight game and his views had to be respected. His track record of developing champions bore evidence of this. A swimmer may look good swimming the length of the pool, but that does not mean they are ready to take on the Channel. Bruno was not yet ready to take on the equivalent of the Channel in the boxing ring.

Stewart Lithgo

Bruno resumed ring duties on 18 January 1983 at the Royal Albert Hall, when he took a step up in class to face the experienced Stewart Lithgo—a man who had fourteen wins, three defeats, and two draws to his credit. Lithgo had won the Northern Area heavyweight championship on 26 November 1981, outpointing holder George Scott over ten rounds. Lithgo was not devoid of ambition, and, while no one thought for one minute that he would beat Bruno, he looked more capable than previous opponents of extending Bruno.

Lithgo had his own British title aspirations halted on 21 February 1982 when Gordon Ferris stopped him in two rounds in an eliminator for the British heavyweight title. Should he beat a budding prospect like Bruno, he would be back in the mix for the championship, so he had plenty of incentive to win the bout. Prior to fighting Bruno, Lithgo had drawn over eight rounds with Maurice Gomis in France on 18 November 1982.

Lithgo was really up for the fight and attacked quickly when the contest got under way, landing with some jabs—but Bruno got through with solid, hurtful digs of his own. Lithgo was not deterred and went about his task with relish, not shying away from Bruno and often forcing him to the ropes. Lithgo's commitment to the fight could not be faulted, as he took a couple of blows that were not what could be called innocuous.

The second round proved to be an exciting one, with both men swapping punches and Lithgo catching Bruno with a number of his own shots. It started to look as if Bruno had a real fight on his hands and was up against an opponent who was going to take him further than he previously had in a contest that was slated for eight rounds.

The third session, once again, was one to savour and enjoy, with both men giving the spectators some exciting action. It was much the same in the fourth stanza; Lithgo was standing his ground and landing with a number of his own shots. The said round maintained the action, with both men freely letting their punches go. However, at the end of the fourth session, Lithgo's corner called the referee over to advise him that they were retiring their fighter due to bad cuts above and below his left eye—damage that Bruno's heavier shots had caused during the contest. Lithgo was not happy about the decision, but he accepted the defeat with good grace. Had it not been for the cuts, Lithgo would have pushed Bruno into later rounds, but the undefeated fighter was looking stronger as the fight continued, and would have most certainly halted his opponent eventually, landing one of his right crosses or left hook to end the bout. At that stage, Lithgo had proven to be Bruno's most competitive opponent in the professional ranks.

This was not the end of the road for Lithgo. He would go on from this defeat and, on 14 May 1984, create a little ring history of his own in the weight division below heavyweight: putting his name in the record books as the first man to win the Commonwealth cruiserweight championship, stopping Australian Steve Aczel in round eleven at the Festival Hall in Brisbane, Queensland.

Peter Mulindwa Kozza

Raring to go, Bruno made another visit to the Royal Albert Hall on 8 February 1983 in a ten-round bout, and yet again made short work of the fighter in the opposing corner. This time it was Peter Mulindwa Kozza of Uganda who felt the full power of Bruno. Kozza brought a very modest record of just 7 bouts to the contest, which suggested that he would be chopped down well before the final bell had sounded. The Ugandan had won three, lost two, and drawn two of his previous ring outings.

Not surprisingly, Kozza found that he could not cope with the punch velocity Bruno brought to the ring and was duly knocked out in the third round. The man from Uganda was outgunned and outfought from the start of the contest; Bruno was able to penetrate his defence and land his damaging blows to register his win.

In fairness to Kozza, he had taken the contest at short notice to replace the original opponent, reportedly former world title challenger and European heavyweight king Alfredo Evangelista, who pulled out of the contest due to an injury. The meeting with Evangelista would have been a more meaningful fight for Bruno had it taken place.

Winston Allen

Bruno once again boxed at the Royal Albert on 1 March 1983 against Welshman Winston Allen, an experienced fighter who had composed a record of twenty-two fights, winning eleven and losing eleven. There was only going to be one winner in a bout scheduled for ten rounds, and that was not going to be Allen.

At that moment in time, Wales had produced five fighters who had gone on to win the British heavyweight crown, said boxers being Jack Petersen, Tommy Farr, Johnny Williams, Joe Erskine, and Neville Meade. Farr had the distinction of having challenged the great Joe Louis for the world heavyweight crown on 30 August 1937 in the USA, losing a competitive fifteen-round points decision that drew him great acclaim for his effort against a champion who was heading for greatness.

Allen was obviously nowhere near the class of the aforementioned fighters, however, he was a man who always came to fight, and hence would always give his best when in the ring. Bruno was expected to win, but it was hoped that he just might be pushed a little by the Welshman and given a few problems to overcome along the way.

It was not to be. Allen was out of his league from the start, but he did land a couple of right hands on Bruno's chin, which suggested for a brief moment that this just might prove to be a telling battle after all. However, he did not have the necessary power to topple, or even inconvenience, the undefeated hope in any way. Yet he was a good choice of boxer for Bruno to meet, considering Allen's past record.

Allen had mixed with a number of good names during his time. In his last bout on 28 October 1982, he had fought Joe Bugner, the former British, European, and Commonwealth heavyweight king, losing when knocked out in round three. When measuring the respective performance against Bugner's, it was more than just a little encouraging to see that Bruno did the job quicker, stopping his man with ultimate ease in round two.

These wins, even against opponents who he was more than expected to win against, added fuel to the reputation of Bruno, which was growing stronger with each bout. Bruno was a proven puncher, and if there is one thing the fans love, it is a puncher who can put his man to sleep early. Even the Americans were now casting an interested and curious eye on this latest hope from the UK, wondering if he was a false alarm or the real deal. Could Bruno be, at long last, the Briton capable of standing up to top American opposition on equal terms and, in so doing, shaking up the division and bringing the world heavyweight crown to the UK?

A British fighter who was a genuine world title threat in the division would, without any question, generate a great deal of interest—especially if he could deliver the goods when called upon to do so and hence win that big prize.

While all the attention and publicity was very flattering, it was, by its very nature, putting added pressure on Bruno. Such pressure can often be counter-productive to a young fighter.

Eddie Neilson

On 5 April 1983, in his fifth consecutive appearance at the Royal Albert Hall, Bruno met the useful Eddie Neilson. Neilson had a professional record of thirty-five bouts with six defeats, and was a dogged fighter who could not be taken lightly. Indeed, at an earlier stage during his career, Neilson looked to be a performer of promise—not a potential world-beater, but a prospective future British heavyweight title challenger.

In his last contest, which took place on 9 December 1982, Neilson (like Bruno's previous opponent, Winston Allen) had faced and duly lost to world title challenger and former British, European, and Commonwealth heavyweight champion Joe Bugner, having been stopped in the fifth round. Neilson still had ambition, and was confident that he could derail the Bruno express and put life back into his own career. Whatever the outcome, it appeared that Bruno's latest foe had enough know-how to make it an interesting night and perhaps give the undefeated Londoner a testing time by taking him to a few rounds.

However Neilson, who fought in the southpaw stance, found Bruno's phenomenal punching power hard to stand up to, and found the canvas three times in the opening round. Such was the way Bruno was attacking his man, landing big blows to fell Neilson, it looked as if it might all be over in the opening stanza. The badly stunned Neilson survived and even saw out the second session after taking more punishment from Bruno—even fighting back and attempting to turn the tide. Neilson, while putting on a brave display, was eventually stopped in the third stanza, having been put on the canvas once more by Bruno. The finishing punch, a big right hand, landed forcefully, convincing the referee that it was time to bring the exciting bout to a close. Neilson showed the damaging signs of battle, finishing the contest with a badly cut right eye. Neilson gave his all, but it was apparent from the off that the contest was not going to last ten rounds with Bruno in such fine attacking form. This looked good for Bruno, since he had once again outshone Bugner, defeating Neilson even faster than he had.

Scott LeDoux

It was now time to move up to yet another level and, on 3 May 1983, the British fighter stepped into the ring at Wembley Arena to meet American Scott LeDoux, who had a record of forty-nine bouts with twelve defeats and four draws. The former two-time world heavyweight champion Floyd Patterson sat ringside with TV commentator Harry Carpenter to observe the British fighter in action. Patterson had given Bruno some valuable tips in the gym prior to this contest.

LeDoux was an experienced professional who had shared the ring with a number of class fighters, like former world heavyweight king George Foreman, who had stopped him in three rounds on 14 August 1976. On 22 October 1977, LeDoux entered the ring with future world heavyweight champion Leon Spinks in a contest that resulted in draw over ten rounds. Ron Lyle outpointed LeDoux over ten rounds on 12 May 1979 in a hard-fought bout. A meeting with former WBC world heavyweight title holder Ken Norton ended in a ten-round draw on 19 August 1979. Future WBA world title holder Mike Weaver took a twelve-round points decision over LeDoux on 24 November 1979 in a contest for the USBA heavyweight title. A bout with future WBA world heavyweight king Greg Page, who was defending the USBA heavyweight crown, concluded with a fourth-round stoppage defeat for LeDoux on 11 December 1981. LeDoux crossed gloves with future WBA world heavyweight title holder Gerrie Coetzee, but suffered an eighth-round knockout defeat on 27 March 1982. LeDoux had also made a futile challenge for Larry Holmes's WBC world heavyweight crown on 7 July 1980, being stopped in round seven.

There was no denying that LeDoux came off second-best more often than not when confronting said fighters. Yet his experience, and the fact that he had faced such class fighters, was evidence that Bruno would hold no fears for him. While it was true that LeDoux was battle-worn, he was a good gauge by which to measure the Briton's progress to date. It should also be remembered that fighters like LeDoux can be very dangerous, for they are always looking for the big win to put them back in the big league and, in turn, in line for big money fights. Bruno's reputation was now making him a target for such opponents, since anyone who defeated the Briton, who was fast becoming the golden boy of British boxing, would most certainly escalate a few steps up the rankings—a fact LeDoux was more than aware of.

Stepping into the ring, all the pressure was on the British fighter, who was expected to do well. From the first bell, Bruno went to work with a cool confidence and composure, constantly scoring with his thumping left jab to LeDoux's face—even flooring him for a count before the bell sounded to end the first round. This was good exciting stuff and the fans lapped it up, giving the home fighter their support with howls of encouragement. The next session brought no joy for the American as Bruno dominated, putting in a sensational performance. Round three of the contest, which was set for ten, proved to be the last, when the referee stepped in to stop the bout due to a bad cut over LeDoux's left eye.

Once again, the British fighter looked impressive in victory, taking his undefeated record to fifteen, with every win having come inside the distance. The future was looking brighter and brighter.

Barry Funches

Bruno increased his undefeated run when Barry Funches of the USA became yet another victory on his record on 31 May 1983, being stopped in the fifth round at the Royal Albert Hall. Funches represented less of a threat than LeDoux and did not look likely to be the first to take the scalp of the British prospect. Funches had a record of eighteen fights, winning eight, losing nine, and drawing one of his contests.

The American had fought on UK turf before, losing on points over eight rounds at the Wembley Arena on 30 March 1982 against former British heavyweight king, Gordon Ferris. Funches had fought some good opposition, but with little success. On 23 October 1980, he lost a ten-round points decision to future WBA world cruiserweight king Ossie Ocasio. John Tate, the former WBA world heavyweight champion, stopped him in round seven on 15 October 1981. Then, prior to meeting Bruno, Funches was stopped in round eight by Eddie Gregg on 14 January 1983.

Funches was not going to keep Bruno awake at night prior to their ten-round meeting. The American did not have the punching power or boxing ability to stave off any attacks by Bruno for the full duration of the contest. The win by the Briton proved very little, but the bout did help to maintain Bruno's ring sharpness and help him stay concentrated. Funches had to be given a degree of credit for taking Bruno the furthest he had been in a contest to date. What it added to his actual boxing education is somewhat debatable, since Bruno was able to dictate throughout the contest without ever being put under any kind of pressure by his opponent. However, it was clear that this was a marking-time fight while possible bigger plans were devised for Bruno's future.

Mike Jameson

In the song 'My Kind of Town', singer Frank Sinatra sang about the merits of Chicago. The next stop for Bruno was the USA, and he plyed his trade there on 9 July 1983; showing that, just like the blue-eyed Frank, Chicago was his kind of town. Bruno confirmed this not through the power of song but through the power of punch, when he impressed by knocking out American Mike Jameson in two rounds.

Bruno and Jameson were matched in a bout slated for ten rounds at the Di Vinci Manor. While Jameson was a worthy adversary, a professional who possessed a record of sixteen fights, eleven wins, and five defeats, the simple truth was that he had no pretentions of being a world class fighter, and was once again no real threat to Bruno. No one expected Jameson to upset the applecart and it would have been a massive shock had he done so.

However, taking the British fighter to battle in the States was a clever move and a worthy exercise since it gave him vital experience and a valuable insight into competing in the country that had produced many top heavyweights over the years—and would obviously play a significant role in his career at a later date.

A few years later, Jameson stepped into the ring with the then red-hot prospect Mike Tyson on 24 January 1986 at the Trump Plaza Hotel in Atlantic City. Like Bruno, Tyson was an undefeated fighter taking part in his seventeenth contest when he faced Jameson, and was building a reputation as a ruthless puncher who blasted his opponents out easily. Nonetheless, Jameson lasted into the fifth round with Tyson before being stopped. The fact that Bruno had halted Jameson quicker than Tyson put him into a good light.

The night in Chicago proved to be an eventful one not just for Bruno, but for two other UK fighters who joined him on the fight card. British welterweight title holder Lloyd Honeyghan continued to show his potential by stopping his American opponent, Kevin Austin, in round ten. British featherweight king Barry McGuigan added to the trio of win's by knocking out another fighter from the USA, Lavon McGowan, in round one.

Bill Sharkey

Busy Bruno's next bout took place at the Wembley Arena on 27 September 1983 against another boxer from the United States, Bill Sharkey, who had won twenty-two of his previous fights, losing six, and drawing one. Two of the opponents who stood out on Sharkey's record were future WBA world heavyweight king Mike Weaver, who outpointed him over ten rounds on 1 April 1977, and a ten-round draw against Scott LeDoux on 26 September 1978.

It was clear that the visitor from the USA was not a risky opponent and was not going to be the monsoon to douse the flames of Bruno's success. In fact, Sharkey provided very little in the way of opposition, as he was dispatched in the first round of a ten-round contest by being knocked out.

This bout was a disappointment to some critics, a number of whom still held the firm, unrelenting view that fighting this kind of opposition was not going to extend or test Bruno in any way whatsoever. The overall feeling was that Bruno was only really padding out his record with soft touches, giving a false impression of his abilities. It was further concluded that the time was now well overdue for Bruno to step up a level and fight an opponent of substance: one who would not buckle easily under pressure and fight back to really test the British hope. This, it was argued, had to happen if Bruno was going to be taken seriously as a future contender for the world heavyweight championship. In Bruno's defence, it has to be taken into consideration that the Briton was still very much a novice in the punch-for-pay ranks and it was vital not to rush him too quickly, since this could result in a damaging defeat. The ring can be a dangerous place, and a fighter should not be matched with an opponent of a higher class until his management feel that he is ready to take on such an assignment.

On the same card, another Terry Lawless fighter was in action and he proved to be less than successful when he suffered an unexpected setback. Charlie Magri had won the WBC world flyweight title on 15 March 1983, stopping Eleoncio Mercedes of the Dominican Republic in seven rounds. Magri was making his first defence of the championship against challenger Frank Cedeno of the Philippines. Cedeno was considered no easy task, but it was generally felt that the hard-punching Magri would emerge the victor at the end of the night—Cedeno provided a shock when he stopped Magri in round six to become the new champion.

Bruno was able to observe first-hand, if he did not already know, just how painful the sport can be to both body and mind, be it at flyweight or heavyweight.

Floyd Cummings

Floyd 'Jumbo' Cummings was the next man to share the ring with Bruno at the Royal Albert Hall on 11 October 1983. Cummings had participated in twenty-one bouts, winning fifteen, losing five, and drawing one.

This was a genuine step up in class for Bruno. The two most interesting results on Cummings's record were his ten-round draw with former world heavyweight champion Joe Frazier on 3 December 1981, and a ten-round points defeat against future WBC and WBA world heavyweight title holder Tim Witherspoon on 16 July 1983. The draw against Joe Frazier looked good, since this was the fighter who had first defeated Muhammad Ali in the professional ranks by a fifteen-round points decision, in a world title bout contest that took place on 8 March 1971. Joe was regarded as one of the greats in the heavyweight division. However, it should be remembered that this was not the Frazier of old, but a fighter on the come-back trail, on whom time and hard fights had taken a heavy toll. Yet this bout against Cummings looked a good match for Bruno, and one that would test the Briton more severely than he had been to date. In doing so, it would answer the critics' questions about his potential. The only time that Cummings had been defeated inside the scheduled distance was by Jeff Sims in a contest that had taken place on 2 May 1982, which ended by way of a stoppage in round eight. Cummings would not fold easily in the heat of battle, and there was every indication that he could stand up to Bruno's punches.

Based on the form book, this was a fight that Bruno should win—certainly a betting man would not consider it a risk to put his house on Bruno punching his way to victory. Cummings, it had to be said, had a little more about him than the Briton's previous opponents, and appeared to be a fighter who could test Bruno's resolve to the full. Cummings was a tough man in and outside the ring, as he had learned how to box while serving a jail sentence.

The American gave clear signals that he was not in the UK just to sip tea or to sample our fish and chips. He was not a tourist keen to see the Tower of London or Buckingham Palace; he was here on business, and he took that business very seriously. A win over Bruno would do his career no end of good; he had little to lose and a lot to gain, which made him a dangerous foe. Cummings had been in with hard-punching fighters before, so in no way would he fear Bruno.

Bruno started the ten-round contest well, confidently using his left jab to push the aggressive American back. The watching fans could be forgiven for thinking that this was going to be another early night for Bruno. Yet a storm can suddenly take place even on a calm sea, and a nasty shock was in store for the home fighter. Just before the bell sounded to end the first round, Cummings caught Bruno with a crunching right to devastating effect.

The British fighter looked out on his feet. Bruno was duly assisted back to his corner, where all efforts were made to revive him for the next stanza. It really looked as if the Bruno bubble was well and truly about to burst, and that he was going to meet with defeat for the first time in the paid ranks. This was a reminder that it takes just one punch to turn the tide in a fight; one punch to change the direction of a fighter's career. Many watching the fight feared that the second round would see Cummings finish his man and take a good victory back with him to the USA. If anyone had put their house on Bruno to win, it looked at that moment to have been a most unwise investment and they had better start looking for a new abode.

When Bruno came out for the next session, the American attacked, looking for what he felt was certain victory. Cummings, emboldened by his earlier success, rained punches with fierce intent on his now-vulnerable opponent. To his credit, Bruno somehow rode out the problematic moments and was able to last out the round. Throughout the rest of the contest, the British fighter stayed calm and picked his punches with precision to steadily take control. However, there was still the concern that Cummings just might find his way through Bruno's defence and connect with another blow to land the win.

Then, in the seventh round, much to the relief of the many spectators in attendance, Bruno found the target and landed the damaging punches to floor his man and force the referee to stop the bout. For the first time Bruno had been in difficulties in his professional career, but it was good to see that he revealed a fighter's heart to survive the crisis and fight his way to victory in what had been his hardest professional outing to date.

Nonetheless, it did raise a worrying question about his chin and his ability to take a punch. Some pundits stated that Bruno was lucky: had he been caught earlier in the round, Cummings would surely have had sufficient time to finish him off either by a knockout or by the referee's intervention. While that may have been true, the same can also be said about the contest that took place at Wembley Stadium in England on 18 June 1963. An up-and-coming American by the name of Cassius Clay (later Muhammad Ali) found himself on the canvas in round four after sampling the left hook of the then reigning British and Empire heavyweight champion, Henry Cooper, just before the bell sounded. Had Cooper caught his man earlier during that round, it is possible that he might well have stopped his badly shaken foe and changed the face of boxing history. It was more than obvious that Clay was hurt and ready for the taking—another blow from Cooper's left hook would have put paid to the brash, undefeated American, and brought the fight to an end. The future three-time world heavyweight title holder recovered, however, and came out to stop a badly cut Cooper in the fifth stanza. Was Clay lucky? Was Bruno lucky? Maybe they both were, but that is the way the cookie crumbles. Luck can play a large part in boxing, just as it often does in life.

There would clearly be sterner tests ahead for Bruno against bigger punchers, and without doubt the now-nagging question about his ability to take a punch would be answered in the fullness of time.

Walter Santemore

After the Cummings scare, Bruno was back in the ring at the Royal Albert Hall on 6 December 1983 in a contest set for ten rounds against the American Walter Santemore, who was armed with a record of thirty-three bouts, winning twenty, and losing thirteen. Santemore was a reasonable enough opponent without being a threat to the Briton; he was not likely to land a punch on Bruno's whiskers and shake him up the way Cummings had previously done. Bruno did not need such a scare again—if the Cummings fight had put a slight dent in his confidence, Santemore looked to be the man to restore it.

Santemore's best-ever victory in his professional career had been a ten-round points decision on 17 August 1982 against Earnie Shavers. Without doubt, this was the high point of his career, one that made people sit up and take a little notice, perhaps thinking that Santemore looked like a fighter who could produce the goods. This was a fair enough assumption since Shavers was a respected fighter and one of the hardest punchers in the division during his time—a man who might well have won a version of the world championship had he fought in another era.

During his peak years, Shavers had shared the ring with the best the division had to offer: men like Jimmy Young, who he stopped in three rounds on 19 February 1973, and boxed to a ten-round draw in a return bout on 26 November 1974. Jimmy Ellis, the former WBA world heavyweight king, was quickly defeated by Shavers, whose potent fists put him away in round one on 18 June 1973. Jerry Quarry turned the tables on 14 December 1973 when he chilled Shavers in round one. It was another one-round finish on 23 March 1979, when the former WBC world heavyweight title holder Ken Norton was put away in said stanza by Shavers. Joe Bugner was halted by the American in the second round on 8 May 1982.

Shavers had also fought twice for the world heavyweight championship. On 29 September 1977, he challenged and failed to win the undisputed crown from Muhammad Ali, losing a fifteen-round points decision. The second bid took place on 28 September 1979, when he went up against Larry Holmes for the WBC version of the title. On this occasion, he was stopped in round eleven.

At first glance, the recorded win by Santemore over Shavers looked pretty good, maybe even stunning. However, on a much closer examination of his record, it had to be said that the victory came in the autumn of Shavers' boxing career, and he was unlikely to see another summer. Santemore was not going to put Bruno's name in his win column since his interest in the contest ended when knocked out in round four. It was not a difficult night for Bruno; just another day at the office and another step towards the much sought-after world title challenge.

Juan Antonio Figueroa

Bruno started 1984 with a contest on 13 March at the Empire Pool, Wembley, where his opponent was Juan Antonio Figueroa from Argentina. The fighter entered the fray armed with a record of twenty-six bouts, winning twenty, losing five, and drawing one. While Argentina has produced its share of worthy gloved men, it was obvious that Figueroa was not another boxer from that South American country who could be cast in the much-respected mould of world-class fighters like Luis Ángel Firpo or Oscar Bonavena. During his period in the paid ring, Firpo had challenged Jack Dempsey for the world heavyweight crown on 14 September 1923 in the USA, and had given the American title holder a great deal of trouble before being counted out in round two of an exciting battle in which both fighters paid a visit to the canvas during the short time the contest lasted. Oscar Bonavena stepped into the ring with Joe Frazier on 10 December 1968 for the New York version of the heavyweight championship and failed in his bid, losing a fifteen-round points decision.

Figueroa was clearly going to provide Bruno with another path to victory. In fact, had they played the hit Queen record, 'Another One Bites the Dust' when Bruno walked to the ring that night, it would have been more than appropriate for the occasion. Figueroa was knocked out in the first of a ten-round contest. Had someone quickly looked away in the course of a conversation or any other such relevant distraction, they would have missed the bout.

James Smith

On 13 May 1984, Bruno stepped once more into the ring to face yet another American fighter in the shape of James Smith, nicknamed 'Bonecrusher'. Smith had a record of fourteen bouts with just one defeat, that setback taking place in his professional debut on 5 November 1981 against fellow countryman James Broad, who knocked him out in round four. One victory of note by Smith took place on 30 January 1982, when he outpointed Ricky Parkey over six rounds. Parkey proved to be a good fighter, going on to win the IBF world cruiserweight crown on 25 October 1986, stopping holder and fellow American Lee Roy Murphy in round ten. Smith looked a creditable opponent, but did not appear to have the ammunition to trouble the home fighter. The contest nonetheless pleased the various critics, who felt that Bruno had, at last, climbed into the ring with a man who could test his mettle to some degree and therefore measure his progress in the professional ranks. Prior to the match against Bruno, Smith looked very relaxed and confident about the outcome of the bout, feeling that he was the man to end Bruno's winning run.

The fans at the Empire Pool, Wembley, were also confident—confident that Bruno would notch yet another victory. Their optimism looked well-founded when the bout got underway; Bruno came out of his corner sharply, looking for his opponent and looking good in the early rounds of the bout. Bruno picked his punches well, with his left jab constantly finding its target, followed by a number of solid blows to the head and body of Smith. At this stage it could be said that the British fighter was delivering the goods, boxing like a genuine world-class operator. Bruno appeared to be on another level, a much higher one than his American opponent. To his credit, Smith sucked it up and absorbed Bruno's heavy punches without showing too much distress. The American showed a steely durability and in the process had taken Bruno to the tenth and final round—uncharted waters the British fighter had not travelled in to date. Despite the experience of boxing more rounds in a contest than he ever had previously, Bruno looked to be heading for another win on his record, albeit on points, but that would not be a bad thing since going the full route would give Bruno the experience of pacing himself over the scheduled distance. Even known punchers like Joe Louis, Jack Dempsey, Rocky Marciano, Joe Frazier, and George Foreman could not stop everyone inside the distance. All Bruno had to do to get the win was stay on his feet and last the final stanza, since he had the points securely in the bank. Victory would be his once the bell had sounded to end the round.

It looked like Bruno had it in the bag. Then, Smith turned what looked like an obvious defeat into victory when he threw a left hook that landed on Bruno's jaw, unhinging him from his senses. For a few moments, Bruno was pinned against the ropes while a torrent of punches rained down on him until, eventually, he fell to the canvas to be counted out by the referee.

The outcome might have been different had Bruno grabbed and held in an attempt to smother the attack of his opponent, or if he had he gone down to the canvas and taken a count of eight while on one knee before rising to continue the battle. Either survival tactic would surely have bought him valuable time to let his head clear and, hopefully, hang on until the end of the round. It is, of course, easy to be clever on the safe side of the ropes, but it is not so easy to be clever when in the battle zone being blitzed by damaging blows to the head.

Smith had provided a massive shock on the night and silenced the chants that were ringing out for Bruno. There was a moment of disbelief among all those who witnessed the spectacle. Bruno fans were left dumbstruck—could it really be over for the fighter who was thought to be Britain's best hope in years for the world heavyweight championship? It may have seemed a little on the pessimistic side, but truthfully many critics felt that it was. The veteran scribes had seen it all before—the undefeated British hope destroyed by a useful, well-schooled American. When it came to domestic heavyweights, it appeared that one need only look at the past to predict the future.

Even the Briton's keenest fans would have had to agree that the future for Bruno, with regards to his world title ambitions, did indeed look bleak at this stage, following the defeat against the American. Any big plans for Bruno were now in tatters. After twenty-one straight victories, the British fighter had suffered his first professional defeat. He had been exposed, and all pretensions of his being a world-class heavyweight fighter cruelly ripped away in an instant by Smith. The suspicions about his suspect chin and his inability to take a punch came to the surface, just as they had when Jumbo Cummings caught him in their respective match and almost put his lights out.

It was not all doom and gloom. There were, of course, a number of options still open for Bruno. He could lower his sights and still win the British, European, and Commonwealth titles—in fact, he would be a certainty to do so if the decision by his management team was to go in that direction.

There are bad days, and this was very much one for Bruno. The history of the world heavyweight crown showed other fighters in the past who had bounced back from defeat, often that much wiser and better for their experience, going on to eventually claim the title. Even boxing great Joe Louis suffered a stunning setback on the night of 19 June 1936. On that occasion, former world heavyweight champion Max Schmeling of Germany, who was considered past his prime and not threat to the young Louis, showed that he should not have been written off without a hope when he provided a shock by knocking out the undefeated American in round twelve. Schmeling thus took away the undefeated record of Louis, which then stood at twenty-four. The following year, on 22 June 1937, Louis won the heavyweight crown from holder James J. Braddock, knocking him out in round eight. Louis also gained sweet revenge when, on 22 June 1938, he defended his crown against Schmeling, who retired in the first round of the title bout.

Of course, this is not to say or even suggest for one moment that Bruno and Smith were in the same league as Louis and Schmeling, but it was an example that defeat does not always mean that the game is over. Fighters can come back from a loss, sometimes better than before.

However, many naysayers had now written Bruno off with regards to his world title ambitions. They questioned his durability, stating that he had a less-than-granite chin and clearly could not take a punch, which was his Achilles' heel. The final conclusion was that Bruno was just another British hope who, when put to the test, could not cut it on the world scene. This was a little harsh because anyone caught with a powerful enough punch can be taken out of the fight, granite chin or not.

In hindsight, the loss to Smith was not as bad as it first appeared, since the American proved to be a good fighter who went on to be a force in the division. In his next bout after the Bruno victory, he challenged reigning IBF world heavyweight king Larry Holmes on 9 November 1984, putting in a more than capable performance before being stopped in round twelve by the champion.

On 12 December 1986, Smith provided another shock when he knocked out defending champion Tim Witherspoon in round one at Madison Square

Garden, New York, winning the WBA version of the world heavyweight title. Smith lost the championship with his first defence on a twelve-round points decision in a unification bout with WBC king Mike Tyson on 7 March 1987 at the Outdoor Arena of the Las Vegas Hilton. This was the first time that Tyson had been forced to last the championship distance. So, while Bruno may have lost his undefeated record to Smith, he could at least take heart by knowing that he did so to a future world champion and not a run-of-the-mill boxer. At the tender age of twenty-two years, five months and twenty-seven days, Bruno was still a baby in heavyweight terms. He had the luxury of time, and while the clock was ticking away, it was apparent that it was still very much on his side. He could rebuild his career—the major question now was: would the Smith defeat have any long-term psychological effects?

Ken Lakusta

On 25 September 1984, Bruno answered that question when he eased back into action, facing Canadian Ken Lakusta at the Empire Pool, Wembley. The British fighter looked as good as ever, getting back to his winning ways and showing no signs of being gun-shy after his dramatic, shock defeat by Smith. He knocked out his opponent in the second stanza of a bout set for ten rounds.

In the opening round, Lakusta showed no fear of Bruno, taking the fight to him and even landing a telling punch on his chin. Bruno was not shaken at all by the blow, advancing continuously after his man. Looking for the finish, Bruno exchanged a series of punches with the Canadian. The first round was certainly action-packed, with the Canadian showing that he had come to make a fight of it.

Lakusta had fought future WBC heavyweight king Trevor Berbick in a contest for the Commonwealth and Canadian heavyweight titles on 9 September 1983, losing when knocked out in round ten. The Canadian was obviously not likely to give Bruno his second defeat, with a record of twenty fights, winning fourteen and losing six, but those who knew the boxing game would not have expected Bruno to have been involved in a tough fight so soon after his first defeat.

The fans in attendance were pleased to see Bruno back in the ring and cheered his every move during the contest. Bruno still had a great deal to do establishing himself has a genuine contender for the world crown, but the first brick in the wall had been laid and the foundations looked secure. The win over Lakusta would not cause ripples of excitement in the world of boxing, or indeed have the world-ranked contenders quivering in their boots or running to the hills for cover. However, it was a very good start on the way back for Bruno and a great confidence builder.

Jeff Jordan

The easing-back exercise continued when Bruno met Jeff Jordan in a ten-round contest at the Royal Albert Hall on 6 November 1984. It would be correct to say that no one expected anything less than a win by the home fighter, so it was hardly a surprise when Bruno cranked up the pressure and stopped his man in round three. The American entered the contest with a record of nineteen bouts, winning sixteen and losing three. On the face of it, Jordan's CV looked pretty good, yet it lacked names of real substance, which is often the giveaway when viewing the prospects of a visiting fighter. It soon became apparent, once the fighters came out of their respective corners and exchanged punches, that Jordan did not have the firepower to trouble Bruno in any way whatsoever. It became even more painfully apparent that Jordan was going to leave the ring with an inside-the-distance defeat—and so it proved when the bout was eventually halted, giving the British fighter another victory.

Philipp Brown

On 27 November, Bruno went the full distance for the first time in his professional career, outpointing opponent Philipp Brown over ten rounds at the Wembley Arena. The contest was not particularly exciting—not one to go down in the memory as an epic encounter. Many were expecting fireworks and for Bruno to put the American away inside the distance, so were a little disappointed that he did not do so. It was, in truth, vital for Bruno to get some rounds under his belt. Not all the opposition would fold early when hit, especially those in the upper echelons of the division. While Brown was not what could be called an elite fighter, he was tricky and able to withstand the pressurised attacks made by the hard-punching Briton.

Brown came with a record of twenty-six bouts with twenty-three victories, one defeat, and two draws. In his bout prior to Bruno on 29 September 1984, the American had been stopped by the highly ranked American Gerry Cooney in four rounds. One of Brown's standout victories was over the once world-rated fighter Jimmy Young, winning a ten-round points decision on 29 August 1982. This win looked good on his CV, but in reality Brown had beaten a fighter who was well past his best. Young had become a trial horse for up-and-coming fighters in the division, and this was clearly not the same man who once gave Muhammad Ali a testing night. That testing night for Ali occurred on 30 April 1976; Young lost a fifteen-round points decision when challenging him for the world heavyweight title.

Bruno could not stop Brown as Cooney had, but this did not reflect badly on the Briton's performance. Cooney was a far more seasoned fighter than Bruno and had in his time mixed it with top fighters.

Bruno was now in a no-win situation: if he took the opposition out too quickly, it was criticised by some; if he lasted the full course, he was criticised by others. This only goes to show that it is impossible to please everyone.

Lucien Rodriguez

On 26 March 1985, former two-time European heavyweight champion Lucien Rodriguez was the next fighter to face Bruno at the Wembley Area. The Frenchman looked a good test and was a decent opponent—his record showed that he was more than capable of providing the British hope with a demanding night.

Rodriguez had compiled a record of thirty-nine victories, nine defeats, and one draw. The Frenchman was also a former challenger for the world title, having been outpointed over twelve rounds by then WBC holder Larry Holmes on 27 March 1983. Going the distance with Holmes was an achievement in itself for the Frenchman, since the defending champion had spite in his gloves and could take out a challenger well inside the scheduled distance once his fists landed. Prior to the defence against Rodriguez, Holmes had stopped or knocked out ten of his previous thirteen challengers before the final bell had sounded. Rodriguez had also stood up to the hard-punching Mike Dokes on 10 February 1980 for the full ten rounds, taking all that came his way from the future WBA heavyweight title holder.

Bruno's punches found their target early, resulting in an impressive and empathic first-round stoppage. Rodriguez had been stopped on four previous occasions during his career, but no one had vanquished him as quickly as Bruno had. In boxing, comparisons to another boxer's performance against the same opponent are often misleading and not a true indication of how good the fighter actually is. It is possible, of course, that Rodriguez may have slipped somewhat since he had challenged for the world crown. After the Bruno defeat, Rodriguez took part in just two further contests before hanging his gloves—both fights ended in defeat. Dave Garside from the UK outpointed him over eight rounds on 13 December 1985, then Louis Pergaud from Cameroon repeated the formula on 21 February 1986 by outpointing Rodriguez over the same distance. However, it was still noteworthy and encouraging that Bruno finished Rodriguez early, whereas Holmes had travelled the full distance to notch up his respective victory.

A few weeks earlier at the Empire State Plaza Convention Centre in Albany, New York, a young American boxer by the name of Mike Tyson made his professional debut on 6 March. He stopped his opponent Hector Mercedes in the first round. Tyson had adopted a no-nonsense, ruthless approach to the fight, and even at this early stage of his career he looked to be the real thing—a genuine future star in the division. Tyson would, in the fullness of time, have a significant impact on Bruno's career.

Anders Eklund

Next up on 1 October 1985 was a crack at the European championship held by Sweden's Anders Eklund. This was an important contest for Bruno since a win would put him in a good position to challenge for the world crown. It looked as if a British victory was on the cards as Eklund was a fighter who had taken part in fourteen bouts, winning eleven, losing two, and drawing one. There was not anything special about his record. Two of Eklund's defeats had come at the hands of British fighters: first danger man Noel Quarless, who stopped him in one round on 13 October 1983; then Joe Bugner, who outpointed him over ten rounds on 13 January 1984. It was clear from past performances in the ring that Eklund had found his level and had, in truth, exceeded all expectations by winning the European championship. Eklund was not going to emulate the success of fellow country man Ingemar Johansson, who held this crown twice from 1956–1959 and 1962–1963, and also reigned as world heavyweight champion from 1959–1960.

In facing Bruno, Eklund would be making the first defence of his European crown, which he had won on 9 March 1985 by stopping holder Steffen Tangstad of Norway in four rounds. The only fear for Bruno in this bout was the time he had spent out of the ring since his last appearance. It had been six months and five days since he stopped Lucien Rodriguez, in a fight lasting just the one round. It was wondered if ring rust would be a problem for Bruno and an advantage for Eklund in their meeting.

Bruno started fast in this championship fight scheduled for twelve rounds, landing solid punches that clearly shook the champion in the early stages of the contest. The British boxer had to be one of the hardest punchers Eklund had faced to date. By round two, the Swedish boxer's face had already begun to show the signs of battle and it seemed only a matter of time before the title changed hands. It looked all too easy for Bruno at this stage; he was fully in charge and dictating the fight. The lack of past ring action did not seem to be impeding Bruno in any way, he was both sharp and alert. Eklund was a proud man who attempted to land telling blows of his own, raising his game in an attempt to retain the title and not lose it in his maiden defence. Eklund was aware that he was the underdog in this meeting and regarded as a mere stepping stone for the British fighter, who had his sights set on a world title bout. Had Eklund not held the European crown, the management team behind Bruno would possibly not have even considered the Swedish fighter as a worthwhile opponent for their man. There was little doubt that, had Bruno and Eklund met in a routine ten-round contest, the bout would have been widely condemned by the critics as an easy fight for Bruno—one in which a win would prove to be of little value to the Briton (which on the face of it was true when based on the past performances of the Swedish fighter). The value of the bout, of course, was not the expected win over Eklund, but the gaining of the European belt, which gave the match some credibility. Despite this, the defending champion was not going to roll over without a fight and was determined to prove those who had written him off wrong. A victory over Bruno, especially on the Briton's own turf at Wembley Arena, would do Eklund's career a power of good—if not securing him a world title bout, then perhaps a possible fight in the USA against a rated contender. Eklund, while not a top-ranked fighter, was a brave man who gave his best, but he was clearly unable to compete with Bruno with regards to power, and so it proved when the Briton landed his punches to relieve the Swedish title holder of the championship by a knockout in round four. Eklund would later regain the title on 28 March 1987, knocking out the then holder, Uruguay-born Spaniard Alfredo Evangelista, in round seven.

The win by Bruno over Eklund was clinical and carried out in an efficient and patient manner, which pleased the home fans who had watched the performance. Hopes were once again running high that Bruno might well be a future world champion.

Bruno had become the first British fighter to hold this European crown since John L. Gardner, who reigned from 1980–1981. Coincidently, Gardner was another boxer who had spent the early part of his professional career in the Terry Lawless stable. While Bruno looked superior to any competition in Europe at that time, with the ability to repel any challengers for his newly won championship, he surprised many by relinquishing the title without making a defence. This was, however, a strategic move by the Bruno team.

The task had been achieved; winning the crown made Bruno the kingpin in Europe and helped to lift his profile and world rating. However, professional boxing is not just a sport but a business, and realistically it was deemed that holding on to the title would prove to be something of a hindrance rather than an advantage for Bruno. By giving up the championship, Bruno was now free from any mandatory defences that the European Boxing Union would later order. Bruno could now fully concentrate his efforts on a shot at the world crown rather than being bogged down by challengers for his continental title.

Larry Frazier

Bruno closed out the year with an undemanding two-round knockout of American Larry Frazier in a ten-round contest at the Royal Albert Hall on 4 December 1985. This victory took his record tally to twenty-seven wins with just one defeat.

During the contest Bruno looked fast and accurate, his punches putting the visitor on the back foot for the duration of the first round. Putting an end to the bout in the second stanza, Bruno scored with an impressive body punch that immediately put Frazier on the deck. Frazier was in obvious distress whereupon he rolled over a couple of times, unable to beat the count of the referee.

Frazier was not the original opponent for Bruno. He had been brought in as a replacement for Larry Alexander, also from the USA, who became unable to box after failing a medical.

Frazier may not have been a fighter in the all-action style of another Frazier called Joe, but all things considered, he was not too bad an operator at this level. Larry came into the ring with a tally of twenty-six bouts, winning nineteen, losing six, with one no contest. Frazier had in the past shared the ring with future WBA world heavyweight king Mike Weaver, who he had knocked out in round two on 11 December 1973. On 14 August 1982, he outpointed Floyd Cummings over ten rounds—a fighter well-known to Bruno. Frazier lost a ten-round points decision to future WBA world heavyweight king Greg Page on 12 February 1983. Then, on 30 September 1985, he lost a ten-round points decision to world-ranked South African Pierre Coetzer prior to his bout with Bruno. Frazier had also lost a ten-round points decision to the man he had replaced to fight Bruno, Larry Alexander, in a contest that took place on 11 July 1985. It should be taken into account that it is possible Alexander would have been a sterner test for Bruno had he passed the medical.

Frazier may have been at the stage where he was losing more fights than he won; it would be true to say that he did not represent a real danger to Bruno. However, while Frazier was clearly beatable as his record indicated, he was no mug in the ring. The simple and plain fact is it would have been madness and bad match-making, which in turn equates to bad business, to have put Bruno in with a dangerous opponent when he was so close to a world title tilt.

Gerrie Coetzee

The next engagement for Bruno took place on 4 March 1986 at Wembley Arena against former WBA world heavyweight champion Gerrie Coetzee of South Africa in a contest billed as a final eliminator for the WBA heavyweight title. This was the big one for Bruno, a vital step in his career and the fight he had to win to secure his desired world-championship shot. While Coetzee looked a little past his best, this still looked a risky match for the home fighter since Coetzee was a very experienced boxer who looked more than capable of giving Bruno a headache or two if on form. There was no two ways about it: Bruno had to get past this particular opponent to prove that he was more than worthy of stepping into the ring to contest the championship. Bruno had to up his game and go for it in a big way; he was now at the all-or-nothing stage of his career.

Gerrie had an interesting history, having won the world crown on his third attempt on 23 September 1983 by knocking out American title holder Michael Dokes in round ten. This was a fight Dokes was expected to win, so the victory was some upset by the South African. Previous failed attempts at the championship by Coetzee had taken place against John Tate on 20 October 1979 for the then vacant WBA crown—the American outpointed him over fifteen rounds. Attempt number two by Coetzee took place on 25 October 1980 when the then reigning champion, Mike Weaver of the USA, retained his title in round thirteen by a knockout.

Coetzee, however, was not fated to have a long reign as a world champion since he lost his title in the first defence when Greg Page duly brought the crown back to the States by scoring a knockout in round eight on 1 December 1984. To his credit, Coetzee had also stopped former world heavyweight champion Leon Spinks in the first round on 24 June 1979, and had drawn with future WBC heavyweight king Pinklon Thomas over ten rounds on 22 January 1983.

The South African fighter had a host of other quality fighters on his record, so he was facing the British fighter with impressive credentials: thirty wins, just four defeats, and one draw. In his last bout, which had taken place on 7 September 1985, Coetzee had a useful tune-up when he outpointed the ring-smart American James Tillis over ten rounds. It looked as if Bruno had a hard night's work ahead of him; a late stoppage or a good ten-round points victory would have been a satisfactory result. However, Bruno went quickly after his man once the fight began, flicking his left jab into the face of the South African. Coetzee moved around Bruno and attempted to counter, but fell short and walked on to a solid right hand that put him down briefly for a count. Bruno went after his man looking for the finish, which can sometimes be a foolish tactic, for an opponent who is hurt can be very dangerous. Coetzee was a man who also packed some power in his punches and it was not beyond the realms of possibility that he might land with one of his damaging blows and put Bruno away. Nonetheless, Bruno provided a shock when he found another right hand that said goodnight Vienna to Coetzee. The South African was counted out in the first round. At that moment in time Coetzee may well have wished that he was indeed in Vienna ,rather than in the ring with Bruno on this particular night, since the Briton looked phenomenal. This was without doubt an astounding win—not so much because Bruno had won, but the speed and ease with which he claimed his best victory to date. Clearly, Bruno was now a serious contender for a version of the world heavyweight title.

Tim Witherspoon

The big chance came for Bruno on 19 July 1986 when the reigning WBA ruler, Tim Witherspoon, was lured to Britain to put his crown on the line at Wembley Stadium. While it is always an advantage to challenge for a world title on home turf, the task in front of Bruno appeared to be enormous, since the American champion was an experienced campaigner who had fought many of the leading lights in the division and was also a former WBC world title holder at the weight. Witherspoon, nicknamed 'Terrible Tim', had a record of twenty-six bouts with just two defeats.

Witherspoon had his first tilt at the heavyweight crown on 20 May 1983, losing a close twelve-round points decision to defending WBC king Larry Holmes. Witherspoon gave Holmes a tough night in a fight that confirmed he belonged with the big players in the division and should never be underestimated.

On 9 March 1984, Witherspoon fought Greg Page for the vacant WBC championship, which had been relinquished by Holmes. This time he was on the right side of the twelve-round points decision to take the title. However, his first defence on 31 August 1984 proved to be his last when challenger Pinklon Thomas emerged the victor on points after twelve rounds. A chance for Witherspoon to redeem himself and become champion again took place on 17 January 1986 when he challenged Tony Tubbs for the WBA version of the championship. Witherspoon made the most of the opportunity by outpointing the defending title holder over fifteen rounds (at that time, WBA world title bouts were scheduled over fifteen rounds).

Witherspoon was not a newcomer to UK rings and had punched for pay previously on British soil. His debut in Britain took place at the National Exhibition Centre in Birmingham on 12 October 1985 where he stopped fellow American Sammy Scaff in four rounds. From the evidence presented, Bruno had a difficult task ahead of him, yet optimism was not in short supply. There was the view in some quarters that, while Witherspoon had the edge against Bruno due to his experience against top fighters, the British challenger had the punch to level the playing field and snatch the title. Also, the last three holders of the WBA crown (Gerrie Coetzee, Greg Page, and Tony Tubbs) had lost the crown in their first defence. Was this a trend that Bruno could exploit or was Witherspoon going to break the mould and make a successful defence?

The expectation surrounding the contest was very high with a great deal of media coverage both in the newspapers and on television. Other sporting events appeared to take second place news-wise during the build-up to the fight—the occasion was that big. Bruno was the flavour of the month, the man everyone wanted to interview at that moment in time; he had to be one of the most famous men in the UK. Boxing fans were counting down the days for the clash of Bruno and Witherspoon. It could be said that the excitement was at fever pitch, the highest it had been for some time over a fight staged in the UK.

The Witherspoon-Bruno encounter was the first world heavyweight title contest to take place in Britain since Brian London's ill-fated attempt against Muhammad Ali, who retained the championship by a third-round knockout at Earls Court on 6 August 1966. In that contest, no one really felt that London had any kind of chance against the great Ali, who was far superior in every way during the time the bout lasted. The defeat of London by Ali came as no big surprise to the fans, it was expected. This time, a win in a heavyweight championship fight by a Briton seemed more than possible—it was one the UK fans desperately craved, so the pressure was well and truly on Bruno. There was no doubt that Bruno, with a charismatic personality, had clearly captured the hearts of boxing fans both young and old. In fact, he was the most popular heavyweight from these shores since the days of former British, European, and Commonwealth heavyweight champion Henry Cooper, and box office king Billy Walker—fighters who were the fans' favourites during their peak years. Bruno had the nation behind him on the night. Even those who were not hard-line followers of the sport took an interest in the contest and were wishing the best for the latest challenger from the UK. Make no mistake, winning a version of the world heavyweight crown was a massive achievement for any fighter, but for a Briton to do so would have been very special.

Witherspoon looked, on paper, to be the easier option at the time when going for the championship. The other two rival title holders were Michael Spinks (IBF) and Trevor Berbick (WBC) who, when considering their records at that time, may well have been too awkward, tricky, and dangerous for Bruno. This is not to say that Bruno was getting a free pass or an easy ride with Witherspoon—far from it—the American was going to be a tough nut to crack. Witherspoon had shared the ring with quality opponents the like of which Bruno had yet to face, which was a significant factor in the contest. This being said, often styles makes fights, and the British challenger looked to have the style to be in with a good chance against Witherspoon. Bruno had been chasing the world title dream since the start of his paid career, now he had the chance to claim the prize and make the dream a reality.

Prior to the start of the big fight, fans were treated to the sight of old rivals, former three-time world heavyweight champion Muhammad Ali and former British, European, and Commonwealth heavyweight title holder Henry Cooper, warmly greeting each other in the ring. The appearance of the two living legends added to the magical atmosphere of the night

At the start of the contest, it was encouraging to see that Bruno did not freeze on the big stage. He went about his work with both zest and confidence, his venomous punches found their target with thudding regularity. The fans sent Bruno's name reverberating around the arena, as they liked what they were seeing. The American was able to take the punches that came his way and replied with his own, but his challenger was edging in front. The American stayed calm and showed no signs of panic, moving confidently through the gears. If Witherspoon was Bruno's Everest, then the early stages of the climb looked most promising. Nonetheless, it should be remembered that all mountains have a slippery slope and are never beaten until the top is reached. Bruno still had some way to go before he reached the summit and, as the rounds rolled by, the job was clearly getting that much more difficult—his stamina was tested to the full, along with his capacity to absorb the punching power of his opponent. Witherspoon had been here before, his experience clearly coming into play. He was not going to surrender meekly, if at all; he was a champion and fighting like one. Something had to give and someone had to break—would it be Bruno or Witherspoon?

Sadly, for British fans, it was Bruno. Both combatants were giving and taking punishment, and in round eleven of the hard-fought fifteen-round contest, the curtain came down on the British challenger's bid when the American produced the finishing blows. The referee stepped in to halt the proceedings seconds after the towel had been throw into the ring by Bruno's corner.

It was all over. For the second time in his professional career Bruno had tasted defeat, and it was not easy to digest. It is often said in exercise: no pain, no gain; Bruno had the pain, but none of the gain with regards to winning the world crown. Bruno had to get over this bitter disappointment and fight his way back. On this occasion his dream had turned into a nightmare.

Bruno's fans were deeply disappointed at his defeat. Many felt prior to the fight that at long last Britain had a heavyweight with a real chance of capturing the championship, yet few could have shared the despondency and disappointment Bruno felt at this time. To get back into title contention would not be easy for Bruno, but he had showed in his performance against Witherspoon that he had the right to challenge for a world crown. He had proved a capable and worthy challenger for the title who gave the champion a tough fight. Bruno had the potential to make it, should another chance present itself in the future. Bruno had to garner more experience and work his way once again towards a world championship challenge. For now, British Boxing had to continue its wait for a fighter who was capable of ruling the heavyweight world.

Before the year came to a close, the big news from America was that Mike Tyson had won the WBC version of the world crown, stopping holder Trevor Berbick of Canada in two sensational rounds at the Hilton Hotel, Las Vegas, on 22 November 1986. He exhibited frightening punching power in taking apart Berbick with relative ease. Tyson looked to be a little special—a man who would be most difficult to lodge from the title.

James Tillis

Bruno did not see action again until 24 March 1987 when American James 'Quick' Tillis put on the gloves in the opposite corner at the Wembley Arena. Tillis was one of those fighters who had been around and fought the best mixing with the likes of Earnie Shavers, who he outpointed over ten rounds on 11 June 1982; future WBC world heavyweight king Pinklon Thomas, who stopped him in round eight on 14 August 1982; future WBA world heavyweight title holder Greg Page on 26 November 1982, who he challenged for the USBA crown and was stopped in round eight. Tillis attempted to win the vacant NABF heavyweight bauble on 23 September 1983, but was stopped in the opening round by future WBC and WBA heavyweight king Tim Witherspoon. Former WBA heavyweight champion Gerrie Coetzee outpointed him over the duration of ten rounds on 7 September 1985, and Joe Bugner took a victory over Tillis by a way of a ten-round points decision on 15 September 1986. Tillis challenged for the WBA world heavyweight crown on 3 October 1981, losing a fifteen-round points decision to champion Mike Weaver. The American also had the distinction of being the first man to take Mike Tyson the distance in the professional ranks, which was no mean feat. The meeting with Tyson occurred on 3 May 1986, with Tillis outpointed over ten rounds. Up to that moment in time, the undefeated Tyson had stopped all his previous nineteen opponents inside the distance.

Tillis came into the ring against the Briton with a record of forty-eight bouts, with thirty-six wins, eleven defeats, and one draw. A win over Bruno would certainly give the American's career a significant boost and a path once again to other high profile bouts.

Tillis, while a little battle-weary, was a good test for the British fighter, who was coming back from his world title defeat. Questions had to be answered: was Bruno's desire still there? Was his confidence where it should be? A great deal was resting on this bout. A defeat against Tillis would be a massive setback, putting a final end to any future world title ambitions for Bruno and perhaps even his career in the ring.

The fight aroused a great deal of attention. Ringside was Mike Tyson, the reigning WBC world heavyweight king, sat with Harry Carpenter, who was commentating on the fight for television with Tyson giving his observations on the contest as it progressed. The appearance of Tyson suggested that a good performance by the British fighter might well see him share the ring at a future date with the American. A series of good wins by Bruno would build up interest and might well make such an event more than possible.

From the start of the contest Bruno went after his man, using his left jab to probe for any openings that he might be able to exploit and land his damaging blows. Tillis was a cute fighter, a smart cookie who had learned a few tricks of the trade over the years, and while being pushed back was able to avoid the kind of punches that might have spelled goodnight and thus end his contribution to the contest. Yet Bruno would not be denied. He was a man on a mission and continued to attack his foe relentlessly, landing with thudding blows that sent a spray of perspiration and blood into the air. Tillis had been in wars with some hard-hitting punchers during his time in the ring and this battle with Bruno was no exception. The American tried everything he knew to stem the attacks from Bruno, but was unable to keep him at bay. Bruno was dishing out some heavy punishment. Round five of a bout slated for ten saw the end of the contest when a bloodied Tillis, whose nose and mouth were damaged and streaming blood, was rescued by the referee. Bruno had performed well and was back in the running. Once again, he had his sights firmly set upon the world championship.

Chuck Gardner

Bruno next fought outside of the UK, the destination being the Palais des Festivals in Cannes, France, on 27 June 1987. The venue was a lovely part of the world; those who visit leave with pleasant memories and a deep-rooted desire to return someday. Those who witnessed Bruno's contest against Chuck Gardner would not leave the arena with such pleasant memories. They most certainly would have no deep-rooted desire to watch Bruno in action against an opponent like Gardner again.

There was no doubt that Gardner was a step down in class after James Tillis. The American had a record of thirty bouts, winning twenty and losing ten. Coming into the contest, Gardner had won his last five bouts against mediocre opposition—three of whom were making their professional debut, which put those victories in perspective. It was notable that whenever he crossed gloves with a class opponent, he did not fair too well. On 1 November 1980, future IBF world heavyweight title holder Tony Tucker (in his first paid bout) sent him to sleep with a knockout victory in round three. Future WBC heavyweight champion Trevor Berbick terminated their contest on 31 January 1981 by a stoppage in round four. John Tate, the former WBA world heavyweight ruler, produced a one-round knockout on 27 November 1981. It took Earnie Shavers two rounds on 5 September 1982 to win by a knockout. Thus, Bruno's latest opponent was known to be susceptible to big punchers, and the Briton was a known big puncher. Based on that premise, it looked as if the writing was on the wall for the American before the bell had even rang to start the contest. To say the outcome was somewhat predictable would be an understatement. Gardner's best win by far had taken place on 15 October 1986 when he outpointed Jimmy Young over eight rounds, a fighter who had been a quality performer but by that time was well past his peak and heading towards the end of his career.

The bout with Bruno was optimistically scheduled for ten rounds, but did not go that far since Gardner was destroyed in the opening round in a contest that really was poor by any standards and difficult to defend in any way whatsoever. The victory was achieved by a left hook and did nothing to enhance the Briton's ring education or reputation in any way; the fight was a waste of time for Bruno and the paying customers. There was no disputing the fact that Bruno was on a much higher level than Gardner and should have been sharing the ring with a much better opponent—one who would have at least made more of a contribution to the respective contest. Such opposition might have been acceptable had Bruno been a little wet behind the ears in his tenth professional bout, but this was his thirty-second paid outing and he was a former holder of the European crown and a previous world title challenger. Bruno would have had harder sparring sessions—but a win is a win, and the Briton could only fight who was in front of him on the night. In the uncertain world of boxing one thing was certain: Bruno's journey towards another world title challenge continued.

After the Bruno bout, Gardner did not put the gloves on again until 6 February 1993 when he faced Mike Evans, who knocked him out in the first round. This proved to be his last assignment in professional boxing.

Reggie Goss

Spain is the country that many British holidaymakers flock to in search of the sun, pleasure, and a much-deserved rest. Bruno followed suit, not for a holiday to seek out the sun, but for the business of his second successive contest abroad on 30 August 1987. At The Plaza de Toros de Nueva Andalucía in Marbella, Bruno squared up to American Reggie Goss, who brought with him a record of twenty-three bouts, winning eighteen and losing five.

Goss was an improvement on Gardner, but he was not likely to win and push Bruno backwards in the rankings. Nonetheless, he was a capable fighting man who, in his last contest on 13 June 1986, had fought Mike Tyson, who stopped him in the first round. That was not a disgrace, since many fighters at that time found the prospect of getting past the opening round with Tyson no easy feat. In fact, it was nearly impossible—Goss had become the thirteenth victim to be halted by Tyson in the first session. It was to be hoped that Goss would not be blown over in the first round like Bruno's last opponent.

The British boxer was not able to score a victory as quickly as Tyson, and that really was a good thing since he could not afford to take part in another farcical affair inside the ring. However, Bruno did stop his man in the eighth round of a scheduled ten. While the encounter was not an exciting or, indeed, an exhilarating one, it did give Bruno some rounds, and that alone made the fight a valuable outing.

Joe Bugner

An intriguing match with former British European and Commonwealth heavyweight champion Joe Bugner on 24 October 1987 was next on the agenda for Bruno. Bugner had had his first professional contest on 20 December 1967, which went badly when opponent Paul Brown knocked him out in round three. Bugner recovered and fought his way up the ladder to become a world-ranked contender in the years that followed. Many felt at the time that Bugner had the talent to be a real threat to the top men and even a possible world champion. Sadly, Bugner failed to live up to world champion expectations, but he did prove to be a genuinely world-class operator.

Bugner had an excellent CV of seventy-three bouts, winning sixty-one, losing eleven, and drawing one. Bugner had fought a vast amount of world-class fighters during his career, crossing gloves twice with the great Muhammad Ali. The first time, on 14 February 1973, was a contest that resulted in a twelve-round points defeat; the second meeting took place on 1 July 1975 for the world heavyweight crown, a challenge that failed when Ali retained his championship by way of a fifteen-round points decision. Bugner had also swapped punches with another great in the shape of former world heavyweight king Joe Frazier on 2 July 1973, putting in a commendable performance before losing a twelve-round points decision. Jimmy Ellis, the former WBA world heavyweight king, found that Bugner had a little too much for him when he lost a ten-round points decision on 12 November 1974.

Bugner had found prominence by defeating Henry Cooper on points over fifteen rounds for the British, European, and Commonwealth heavyweight titles on 16 March 1971. While a springboard to better fights, this victory was a poisoned chalice for Bugner since he was not forgiven by a number of fans for beating a man who was much-loved and respected. Cooper had been the best heavyweight in the UK for a number of years; a man who had created a record by winning three Lonsdale belts outright for defending the domestic crown. Cooper was a dangerous opponent, his famed left hook was a sleeping pill for those who felt it. Bugner was able to box his way through the rounds without falling foul of Cooper's fight-finishing blow.

Going into the ring to face Bruno at White Hart Lane in Tottenham, Bugner was clearly an experienced campaigner. Bugner may have had some miles on the clock, but he still had a good engine and could still perform.

After sharing the ring with so many top fighters, Bugner had picked up some good moves and was a very tricky operator. Bugner, in his last contest, had outpointed former WBA world heavyweight king Greg Page over ten rounds in a bout that took place on 24 July 1987. Bugner had the knowledge that a further win here would help him to re-establish himself, putting him back in the major league and the vital big money fights. There was plenty for Bugner, now an Australian citizen, to aim for. A meeting between Bruno and Bugner had been mooted for some months so there was a degree of interest to see if Bugner could give Bruno problems in their meeting. Bugner was confident leading up to the fight, holding the view that he would expose Bruno and come out on top in their clash.

Sadly, the contest scheduled for ten rounds was not exactly one of the most exciting bouts ever witnessed inside the ring, although it was interesting to watch the former hope of British boxing up against the present candidate. Unsurprisingly youth prevailed (as it often appears to do so in such circumstances) when the contest duly ended in Bruno's favour, putting another victory in his win column with the bout stopped in round eight. Some critics once again jumped on the what-did-that-fight-prove bandwagon, stating that at this stage of his career, Bugner had very little left in his box of tools with which to test Bruno. While one can understand that point of view, it should be remembered that even at that time Bugner was a fighter with a great deal of ring-craft who still had ambitions of his own and would have surely taken advantage of any mistakes Bruno made during the contest.

Mike Tyson (I)

Bruno did not enter the ring again until 25 February 1989 for his second crack at the world heavyweight title held by the undefeated Mike Tyson. The two fighters were scheduled to meet in 1988, but due to various problems outside the ring for Tyson, the bout was put back a number of times, which meant that Bruno saw no action during that period of time.

In his last bout before meeting Bruno, Tyson had chillingly dispatched his last challenger Michael Spinks in ninety-one seconds of the first round on 27 June 1988. Spinks was no slouch, having entered his fight with Tyson with an undefeated professional record of 31 bouts. Spinks, a former gold medallist at middleweight at the 1976 Montreal Olympic Games, was not only a former IBF ruler at the weight, but also a former undisputed world light-heavyweight king. In fact, Spinks was a history maker, having been the first holder of the light-heavyweight crown to win the IBF version of the world heavyweight title. Spinks accomplished this when he outpointed holder Larry Holmes over fifteen rounds on 21 September 1985. This was a shock result with many experts having felt before the fight that Holmes would notch up another successful defence. It was also felt that Holmes would take the crown back in a return bout, yet once again Spinks defeated Holmes by way of a fifteen-round points decision in a contest that took place on 19 April 1986. A second defence against Steffen Tangstad on 6 September 1986 saw Spinks retain his crown with a stoppage in round four. Spinks was later stripped of the championship when he signed to meet Gerry Cooney rather than the IBF number-one contender, Tony Tucker. Spinks duly defeated Cooney by an impressive five-round stoppage on 15 June 1987, and the scene was set for a showdown with Tyson. Spinks, while the underdog, was a talented fighter who looked more than capable of giving Tyson a competitive fight. However, he was taken out with ease by Tyson—the man Bruno was to do battle with. If Spinks, with all of his ring credentials that outshone anything Bruno had been able to achieve to date, could not last a round with Tyson, what chance did the Briton realistically have of victory?

Tyson was undoubtedly a fearsome fighter with tremendous punching power who had previously won all thirty-five bouts, with just four going the distance. Tyson, nicknamed 'Iron Mike', was the overwhelming favourite to retain his crown. How could he not be? When considering his past performances inside the ring, Bruno looked to be heavily up against it in their meeting at the Hilton Hotel, Las Vegas. The undefeated champion, Tyson held the WBC, WBA, and IBF versions of the title and was not going to surrender them without a fight. In fact, surrender was not a word associated with the champion at that time nor indeed was the term defeat. The prospect of sharing the ring or even the very thought of attempting to go twelve rounds with a man like Tyson was an intimidating proposition, even for the experienced and seasoned professional fighter. Indeed, it might have been a good idea to include in any opponent's contract prior to the fight that getting into the ring with Tyson could be most harmful to your health.

Twenty-five years to the day, at the Convention Centre, Miami Beach in Florida, a challenger by the name of Cassius Clay (later Muhammad Ali) looked to have an impossible task on his hands when he ventured into the ring to confront the hard-hitting champion, Sonny Liston. Much like Tyson, Liston radiated the aura of a fighter who could not be beaten. Going into the bout with his challenger, Liston had only experienced defeat once in his 36 bouts—on 7 September 1954 when he lost an eight-round points decision to fellow American Marty Marshall. In a return with Marshall on 21 April 1955, Liston gained revenged with a six-round stoppage over his opponent. Liston continued his winning run, mowing down all who stood in front of him; the man looked impossible to defeat. Liston was eventually given his shot at a world title on 25 September 1962 where he ripped the championship away from holder Floyd Patterson with an awesome display of power to win by a one-round knockout.

If some at the time were harbouring the thought that the win by Liston was something of a fluke, they were wrong. On 22 July 1963, in a return with Patterson, he once again destroyed the former champion with a one-round knockout. Clay's chances did not look too good against Liston. In fact, he looked headed for a most painful night—one that most experts felt would end well before the final bell of the fifteen-round contest rang out. Yet Clay showed that the odds can be beaten and hence shocked the world in no uncertain fashion by winning the crown when Liston retired on his stool at the end of round six. While I do not think it would be too disingenuous to state that Bruno was not a second-coming of Ali, boxing did have a number of upsets recorded in its historical pages. Was it possible that this date would see another shock and another chapter added to the list of upsets with Bruno taking the crown? British fans were hoping this would be so.

The first round of the Bruno-Tyson contest produced some exciting moments when the British fighter was floored for a count soon after the bell sounded by a right hand from Tyson. This was not a good start by Bruno, who looked at that moment that he, like Spinks, would have his title challenge curtailed in the opening round. Upon getting to his feet, Bruno fought back, but within seconds was deducted a point by the referee for holding on. He needed that point deduction like he needed a hole in the head; with the worst of possible starts, things were not going the challenger's way.

Then, Bruno hurt Tyson with one of his bombs, which for a brief moment suggested that perhaps—just perhaps—an upset might be imminent. Bruno, while not having exceptional speed, was a prodigious puncher, which always made him a dangerous proposition for any fighter in front of him, even Tyson. Harry Carpenter, who was commentating for television, let his mask of impartiality slip when he was famously heard uttering the words: 'Get in there, Frank'.

For the first time in the professional ranks, the American had clearly been stunned. However, by shaking the champion Bruno stirred up a hornets' nest. Tyson came back, attacking the challenger in the next round with stinging, hurtful blows. Bruno's all-too-brief moment of a possible upset and a road to glory had gone in an instant. All hopes of a British victory were gradually and brutally crushed. In fairy tales the knight often slays the dragon—if Bruno was the knight and Tyson the dragon, the script on this occasion was going to be very different, with the knight defeated. Tyson, with an air of menace about him, continued to attack without any element of mercy as the rounds passed by. Tyson was determined to take his man out, and every bone-jarring punch he threw and landed clearly shook his opponent. Tyson was the hunter and Bruno the hapless prey trying to survive the onslaught. Those who had previously felt that Bruno was unable to take a punch would now need to reconsider that view; Bruno had taken some tremendous blows from Tyson to both head and torso and was still upright, still looking for a way to win, still looking to land the punch that would turn the fight his way and take the championship. Many other fighters more highly regarded than Bruno had been taken out more quickly when tasting the same leather Tyson had thrown at them.

The excited spectators at ringside cheered on the home champion, who was relentless in his task, yet Bruno did not lack support. His loyal fans who had travelled to the USA were also vocal in their support. Tyson, however, continued to move forward like a tank with no reverse gear, destroying Bruno who could not cope with the huge volume of damaging blows coming his way. Tyson was whipping up a hurricane in the ring and Bruno was well and truly caught in the eye of it. The thoughts of a British fighter wearing the heavyweight crown on this occasion were shattered once and for all with the melee coming to its conclusion in the fifth round.

Tyson, as generally expected, stopped a bruised and bloodied Bruno to retain his crown and confirm that he was *numero uno* at the weight. It was a disappointment for the British fans and, of course, for Bruno, but the defeat was by no means a disgrace. Bruno did his best—he even did something few had been unable to do before, by hurting Tyson. However, the big-punching champion proved too much for the British fighter on the night, handing out a clinical beating as he had to the many who to have previously shared the ring with him. Bruno displayed great courage, but the sad truth is courage alone does not win world titles in the ring.

At this moment in time, many experts were of the view that Tyson looked unbeatable and was on his way to becoming ranked among the all-time greats of the division. By the same token, it was felt that Bruno would join a long list of brave challengers who went for the big one and failed. The thought of the British fighter winning the world title in the future did not now seem likely, especially with a man like Tyson at the helm of the division. The Bruno team had to go back to the drawing board, re-think their future strategy, and consider the various options that may or may not have been open to them. There was a great deal to ponder and consider.

On the undercard of the Tyson-Bruno bout, Trevor Berbick and James 'Buster'

Douglas met. Berbick, the Jamaican-born Canadian, had been demolished by Tyson in two rounds on 22 November 1986 when losing the WBC belt in Las Vegas. His opponent was the American 'Buster' Douglas, who duly won a ten-round points decision over the former champion. In winning the bout, Douglas looked a technically good boxer, but not one that special—certainly not a future world champion if his victory over Berbick and some of his past wins were anything to judge by. When Douglas jetted out to face Tyson in Japan on 11 February 1990, few gave him a chance; it looked a routine defence for the champion and a lost cause for the challenger, who would be lucky to last the full course. In essence, it looked a wasted trip for Douglas, who would perhaps be able to take in the sights of Tokyo but little else. He surely was not going to leave the land of the rising sun a world champion. Once again, boxing produced an upset when Douglas sensationally knocked out Tyson in round ten. The unbeatable had been beaten, and now the division looked wide open. Despite his win over Tyson, many felt that Douglas would not reign for long.

John Emmen

After his world title defeat against Tyson, Bruno had to undergo an operation to his right eye to repair a damaged retina, and thus took a period of time off from the rigours of boxing: two years, eight months, and twenty-six days in total. The operation was successful and Bruno was given the green light to resume his boxing career. Prior to his return, many wondered if Bruno would say farewell to the sport and pursue easier options outside of the ring. Nonetheless, Bruno was not looking for easier options—he was seeking the world heavyweight championship, a title he still felt he could win.

The world title situation had changed during Bruno's absence. The world heavyweight championship was now held by Evander Holyfield, who had acquired the crown when knocking out James Douglas in three rounds on 25 October 1990. The WBO belt, a then fledging organisation, was held by another American, Ray Mercer, who won the crown by knocking out Italy's Francesco Damiani in nine rounds on 11 January 1991.

Bruno returned to ring action on 20 November 1991 with a bout against John Emmen of the Netherlands, who was the reigning Benelux heavyweight champion. While Emmen did not have the ring experience of Bruno, he did have a respectable record of eighteen fights, winning sixteen and losing two. It would be stating the obvious to say that Emmen was a step down in class from the likes of Tyson, however, this type of contest for Bruno was to be expected considering the lengthy period of time he had been away from the ring. Truthfully, Bruno did not need to square off in another war against a major contender at that stage of his career; he had to get back into his stride and shake off the ring rust that had gathered during his absence from boxing. Emmen would be an ideal opponent for such a task. While Emmen was a good fighter at European level, one did not need to have been Sherlock Holmes to deduce who the victor would be once the dust had settled. Even Dr Watson could have predicted the outcome of the contest—it really was rather elementary.

Emmen had challenged once for the European heavyweight title on 22 April 1988 against Italian Francesco Damiani, being stopped in three rounds. Damiani later went on to become the first holder of the WBO world heavyweight crown—a title he duly won on 6 May 1989 by knocking out South Africa's Johnny Du Plooy in three rounds. A noteworthy victory on Emmen's record was a ten-round point's victory over Germany's future WBO world cruiserweight champion Ralf Rocchigiani in a bout on 30 September 1989. Rocchigiani thus captured the vacant title on 10 June 1995, stopping England's Carl Thompson in round eleven.

At the Royal Albert Hall, with his batteries fully recharged and raring to go after his hiatus from the ring, Bruno soon got back to winning in style when he stopped his man in the opening stanza of a ten-round contest. The speed of the victory may not have done a great deal to eradicate any ring rust and would not have pleased some of the paying customers who expected to see more of a fight for their money, but it was a vital confidence builder for Bruno.

Jose Ribalta

Bruno's first bout of 1992 took place on 22 April at Wembley Arena against Cuban-born Jose Ribalta, a fighter who had taken part in thirty-nine bouts, winning thirty-one, losing seven, and drawing one. Ribalta was a step up in class from Emmen, but it was ominous that he had lost his last three bouts prior to his meeting with Bruno—first to former WBA and WBC world champion Tim Witherspoon on 19 July 1990 by a ten-round points decision, then to future WBA world heavyweight king Bruce Seldon on 11 January 1991 by a third-round retirement. This was followed later by a ten-round points defeat to Pierre Coetzer on 11 May 1991. When taking his recent form into account, it was painfully obvious that he was on the downward slope career-wise, and his luck was not going to change against Bruno in this contest unless he could dig deep and find something special that he had not revealed of late.

The Bruno-Ribalta bout was set for ten rounds, but one did not need to be a fight expert to predict not just a victory, but a knockout or stoppage win for the home fighter. Nonetheless, it did look as if Ribalta would last a few rounds, perhaps showing a degree of resistance along the way.

From the opening bell, a positive Bruno went on the attack with cool efficiency, tagging his opponent repeatedly with solid punches to the head and body. Ribalta was soaking up too many blows and could not produce anything to deter or even slow down the man in front of him, who was handing out heavy punishment. Bruno was on fire in this contest and looked a million dollars. He closed the show early by knocking out his opponent in round two.

Pierre Coetzer

While many critics may have faulted some of Bruno's previous opponents, they could not complain about Pierre Coetzer of South Africa, who was Bruno's best opposition since his defeat against Mike Tyson in terms of his record. Coetzer was not without ambition of his own; with a ledger of forty-two bouts, winning thirty-nine and losing three. In his last bout, billed as a WBA world title eliminator, on 18 July 1992, he had lost to future world heavyweight champion Riddick Bowe by a stoppage in round seven. Coetzer could not afford another defeat on his record, so a win over Bruno was vital to his career. Likewise, losing was not an option for the British fighter. Without a shadow of doubt this was a make-or-break contest for both men, and as such the pressure on the two fighters was enormous.

Bruno's performance in the ring confirmed that he was still in the championship mix. He came through on the night and scored another inside-the-distance victory at Wembley Arena. The bout, which took place on 17 October 1992, was scheduled for ten rounds and looked at times as if it would go the full route. Coetzer was well-schooled and knew his way around a boxing ring, so was not going to be taken out early by Bruno. On this occasion, Bruno spent more time in the ring than he previously had for some time and was made to work for his win. He got the better of the exchanges during the fight, but Coetzer stayed with the Briton, stubbornly fighting back in the hope that he just might land the conclusive punch that would see him to victory. The referee finally stepped in to stop the bout in round eight, giving Bruno the deserved victory. The South African's corner had also thrown in the towel, knowing that their man had nothing left to give. Coetzer used all his ring savvy on the night, but did not have the necessary firepower to deter the British fighter and was well-beaten when the end came.

After the Bruno contest, Coetzer got back into the saddle and had what could be described as one more lifeline handed to him when he fought former world heavyweight champion George Foreman. On 16 January 1993, at the Reno-Sparks Convention Centre in Nevada, USA, Coetzer once again met with defeat when stopped in the eighth round in what proved to be the South African's last professional contest.

Carl Williams

Bruno once again took to the ring on 24 April 1993 at the National Exhibition Centre in Birmingham against American Carl 'The Truth' Williams, who entered the ring with a record of twenty-six wins, six defeats, and one no contest. It would be true to say that Williams had seen better days in his career and was not likely to spring any nasty surprises, but to his credit he knew his trade and was no lamb to the slaughter. Williams had fought the best and challenged twice for the world heavyweight crown. The first was a credible attempt against Larry Holmes on 20 May 1985 for the IBF crown, which saw him lose a fifteen-round points decision. A second shot at the championship on 21 July 1989 against the fearsome Mike Tyson for the WBC, WBA and IBF titles saw him stopped by a big left hook in the first round. Williams beat the count, but the referee felt he was not fit to continue. At the time, the beaten challenger protested about the stoppage, claiming that it was premature.

Williams had also shared the ring with other good fighters during his career. On 16 February 1986, former WBA heavyweight king Mike Weaver stopped him in round two. In the defence of his then held USBA heavyweight crown on 27 June 1988, he outpointed former WBC heavyweight champion Trevor Berbick over twelve rounds. Williams came unstuck on 8 March 1991 when former WBC and WBA world heavyweight kingpin Tim Witherspoon outpointed him over twelve rounds to snatch his USBA crown. On 20 August 1992, Williams proved too sharp for former WBA world cruiserweight champion Ossie Ocasio, outpointing him over ten rounds. In his last contest prior to meeting Bruno, Williams had been stopped in round eight by future WBO world heavyweight boss Tommy Morrison on 16 January 1993, but not before giving him a few worrying moments. In a bout that provided a great deal of action, Williams was floored for a count in rounds one and three, but he came back in round five to put Morrison on the deck twice and looked as if he might secure a stoppage win himself before the session ended. The opportunity for Williams came and went—he was eventually worn down and out-punched by Morrison.

The American was experienced, and that experience told against Bruno on the night, pushing the Briton into the tenth round whereupon he was finally stopped. Bruno landed a right hook that sent Williams crashing to the canvas. He beat the count, but the referee decided to halt the bout at that stage.

Both men were aggressive in the early rounds, looking to land the telling punches. Bruno could not blow Williams away early in a contest, which may not have been what could be called edge-of-the-seat excitement, but it was not dull by any stretch of the imagination. Williams had a good left jab, which he put to good use. The spectators, along with Bruno soon, sensed that the American was not going to roll over easily. Williams fancied his chances against Bruno and had not arrived in the UK to become a victim. Bruno had a fight on his hands, one that took a dramatic turn when he was cut over the left eye in round three to make his task that much more difficult. It would have been tragic had Bruno been stopped by an eye injury, but thankfully his corner did a good job controlling the bleeding. In such a situation the laceration becomes an obvious target for an opponent to aim for, but Williams was unable to take advantage of the wound. There was a great deal riding on this contest for Bruno—another world title challenge was looming should he punch his way to victory.

The two men continued to freely exchange punches, with Bruno getting the better of the exchanges. Going into the tenth round against Williams did no harm whatsoever to Bruno— those extra vital rounds would be beneficial. Bruno fought well, but the victory did not give an indication that he would prosper well with his intended meeting with Lennox Lewis. Williams, while a decent enough fighter, was way below the class of Lewis—a man who would give Bruno a more testing time. This contest marked the first time Bruno had fought outside London when boxing in the UK.

Lennox Lewis

Bruno still had the burning desire to become a champion of the world and the opportunity for another shot at the title presented itself once again. Since Bruno's last world title fight, changes had taken place at the top; the various titles passed around in the style of pass the parcel. American Riddick Bowe was the reigning WBA and IBF holder having taken the titles on 14 November 1992 by way of a twelve-round point's decision over Evander Holyfield. Tommy Morrison, also from the USA, held the WBO crown having taken the vacant title when defeating former undisputed king George Foreman on points over the duration of twelve-rounds on 7 June 1993. Fellow Briton Lennox Lewis was the WBC ruler, who had attained the crown before Bruno, so a match between the two was a natural pairing.

After a great deal of negotiations, a contest between Bruno and Lewis was signed. The two who had been rivals not just on the world front but also the domestic one were at last to meet. Britain seemed to be in a good place at this time with there being two top men in the division primed and ready to do battle. This contest really caught fire with the public—ardent fans and casual ones were all talking about the fight. Bruno and Lewis mania had hit the UK in a big way; a truly magical moment for British boxing and the fight looked certain to be a box-office hit.

Both Bruno and Lewis were far from complimentary about each other at their press conference prior to the contest, which helped to generate further interest in the fight. The public love a grudge match with an explosive encounter inside the ring, and this bout was shaping up to be such.

The two fighters locked horns on 1 October 1993 in the open air at Cardiff Arms Park in a fight dubbed 'The Battle of Britain'. Once again, Bruno was up against it in his world title bid. Lewis was a former British, European, and Commonwealth heavyweight Champion, and a gold medal winner at super-heavyweight at the 1988 Seoul Olympic Games. A talented fighter with an undefeated record of twenty-three bouts, twenty of them coming inside the scheduled distance (this included one on a disqualification), Lewis would be making his second defence of the championship and had every intention of putting in a good performance in front of the many fans in attendance.

Once the much-anticipated contest got underway, Bruno went to work early, using his left jab to good effect and picking his opponent off. The early rounds suggested that an upset could be in the making and Bruno, in his third attempt, would achieve his dream of becoming a world champion. In the early stages, Lewis appeared a little sluggish and was unable to target his punches. Soon, however, the class and ring-craft of the defending title holder started to see him take steady control of the contest, with Bruno beginning to ship more punishment than earlier in the exciting contest.

In round seven, after unloading a series of heavy blows, it was all over. The referee stopped the bout in the champion's favour while the defeated Bruno went out on his shield with honour and dignity, having given Lewis an unexpected assortment of difficulties. At that time, it did appear that Bruno's world title dream was well and truly over.

In life, most of us have high ambitions, and that is not a bad thing. Often they remain out of our reach despite our efforts—we then come to the realisation that we have to settle for what we have and accept the cards fate has dealt us. It looked very much at this point in time as if Bruno's ambitions were indeed a little too high, and he would have to settle for what he had. That said, life can be strange, full of twists and turns delivering the unexpected, and as the saying goes: 'It ain't over till the fat lady sings.' Bruno might have been aware that the fat lady was singing, but he was also aware that that she had not yet stopped and had a few more verses to go. One never really knows what is around the corner, which proves to be very much the case in the world of boxing.

On that same evening, a Welsh fighter named Joe Calzaghe, who was managed by Bruno's manager Terry Lawless, stopped his opponent Paul Hanlon in the opening round of his professional debut. Calzaghe would eventually leave the charge of Lawless and, in the fullness of time, develop into one of the greats of British boxing, winning the British super-middleweight title and the WBO, IBF, WBC, and WBA versions of the world championship. Calzaghe retired from the sport in 2009 with an undefeated record of forty-six fights, for which he was inducted into the International Boxing Hall of Fame in 2014.

Jesse Ferguson

After being defeated by Lewis, many wondered where big Bruno would go now. Would he give up his desire to win the heavyweight title? Would he continue to box at all, after three failed painful attempts at the world championship? It was proving to be a most elusive, if not impossible title to acquire. Most men would have come to the decision that enough was enough and quit if not the ring, then at least the chase for the championship. However, it was apparent that Bruno was not most men, and certainly no quitter. He still felt it was his destiny to win the title. Bruno may have lost a few battles, but he had not lost the war.

Bruno decided to continue his boxing career and met Jessie Ferguson on 16 March 1994 at the National Exhibition Centre in Birmingham. Ferguson was, on record, a reasonable choice of opponent for Bruno to resume his career with after his defeat against Lewis. Ferguson had engaged in thirty-one bouts, winning twenty and losing eleven, but it must be taken into consideration that the American's defeats had come against a number of top-notch fighters who could be called, without fear of contradiction, the cream of the crop. Ferguson's record included a ten-round points victory over James Douglas, the future world heavyweight king, on 9 May 1985. However, he was not so fortunate in bouts with future world heavyweight champion

Mike Tyson, who stopped him in round six on 16 February 1986; then future WBA world heavyweight champion James Smith, who duly gained a ten-round points decision over him on 7 June 1986. Oliver McCall, the future WBC world title holder, outpointed him over ten rounds on 8 August 1991; future WBA ruler Bruce Seldon defeated him by a five-round retirement on 19 January 1992; Michael Dokes, the former WBA champion, outpointed him over ten rounds on 28 July 1992; and former WBA world title holder Tony Tubbs defeated him by a ten-round points decision on 24 November 1992. Ferguson had also challenged Riddick Bowe on 22 May 1993 for the WBA world heavyweight crown, losing in his bid when knocked out in two rounds. In his bout before meeting Bruno, Ferguson had lost a close ten-round points decision to former WBO heavyweight king Ray Mercer on 19 November 1993—an opponent he had previously outpointed over ten rounds on 6 February 1993.

While Ferguson often lost to the big names when he faced them and could be said to be on a downward trend, it was still felt that, after meeting such exalted company inside the ring, he would last a few rounds with the Briton before tasting defeat. Nobody thought for one minute that Bruno would come out the worst in this meeting. However, Ferguson knew the boxing business and was by no means a novice walking into the unknown.

In a contest scheduled for ten rounds, Bruno showed no ill effects from his defeat to Lewis and was on his game. In no mood to hang around long in the ring, Bruno stopped his man in the first session, attacking ferociously from the off, not giving his outgunned opponent a chance to retaliate. The American took two visits to the canvas before the bout was eventually stopped after Bruno had him trapped on the ropes with a sustained attack. Ferguson, in his entire career, had never been stopped as quickly as this before, which made Bruno's victory look all the sweeter in the light of day. Bruno had now won twelve of his winning bouts in the first round, which was testament to his punching power. Bruno was back; this win over Ferguson was his ticket to more meaningful fights in the division.

Rodolfo Marin

Rodolfo Marin, who hailed from Puerto Rico, was next to face Bruno on 18 February 1995 at the Bath and West Country Showground in Somerset. Marin had a record that looked pretty good at first glance—going into battle twenty-three times, he had won twenty and lost three. The three defeats came at the hands of Tyrell Biggs, who outpointed him over ten rounds on 8

December 1990; the future world heavyweight champion Riddick Bowe, who dismissed him in two rounds by way of a knockout on 28 June 1991; and, in his last bout before meeting the Briton, a ten-round points decision loss to Joe Hipp on 1 November 1994.

The Puerto Rican could not be described as a world-beater in any shape or form, and it was notable that whenever he stepped up a level he met with defeat. However, he was a capable performer who looked as if he might be able to last into the later rounds of a contest scheduled for ten. Nonetheless looks can be deceiving, as the fists of Bruno ended the contest once again in the first round. The fight was a tepid affair, which turned out to be a little disappointing.

At this level, Bruno was unstoppable, but would he be able to look as impressive when he once again stepped up another rung in the ladder or, indeed, if contesting another world title? At that moment, it appeared to be a foolish notion to think that he would receive yet another chance at the world heavyweight crown.

Mike Evans

Bruno's next outing came north of the border, when he laced up the gloves to do battle at the Kelvin Hall in Glasgow on 13 May 1995. At this time, Scotland had yet to produce a British heavyweight champion, although they had contributed a great deal to the reputation of UK boxing by producing a number of world champions: Tancy Lee (flyweight IBU and British version), Johnny Hill (flyweight British version), Benny Lynch (flyweight NBA and British version), Jackie Patterson (undisputed flyweight), Walter McGowan (WBC flyweight), Ken Buchanan (undisputed lightweight), Jim Watt (WBC lightweight) and Pat Clinton (WBO flyweight). This included an impressive host of other Scottish fighters, who may not have held a world crown but became European, British and Commonwealth title holders in other weight divisions. It was very clear that the Scottish fans in attendance knew their boxing, and Bruno was keen to impress them.

The opponent facing Bruno was Mike Evans from America. Evans was a fighter who had met some of the best in the division—men like former WBA world heavyweight king Tony Tubbs, who outpointed him over ten rounds on 20 April 1989; and Tony Tucker, the former IBF world heavyweight title holder who outpointed him over ten rounds on 8 March 1990. Then future WBO heavyweight king Corrie Sanders took a ten-round points decision over Evans on 22 August 1992. Evans once again met with failure when he confronted the former WBO world light-heavy and heavyweight king Michael Moorer on 4 December 1993, going down to a ten-round points defeat. While Evans had lost to these fighters, he had acquitted himself well and in each instance heard the final bell.

Evans had fought in the UK before, on 2 March 1991 at the Dolphin Centre in Darlington, County Durham, outpointing fellow American and former IBF world cruiserweight champion Lee Roy Murphy over twelve rounds to capture the vacant IBF inter-continental heavyweight crown. Evans had put together a record of forty-one bouts, winning thirty, losing ten, and drawing one. In his last bout before confronting Bruno Evans, he had travelled to Sao Paulo in Brazil to face home fighter Adilson Rodrigues on 7 March 1995. Rodrigues was no mug—while he was not a world beater, he was a good fighter. There were no two ways about it: Evans was drafted in to provide the Brazilian with a win on his record. The American was not expected to win, yet Evans stunned the locals by scoring a knockout in seven rounds.

The indication based on past performances was that he would give the British fighter a run for his money, since he had only been stopped twice when defeated in the past. The first inside-the-distance defeat for Evans came against Ricky Reese very early in his career in a contest that took place on 26 August 1983, which resulted in him being knocked out in the first round. The second occasion took place on 25 June 1994 against Jorge Luis Gonzalez in a bout that ended by way of a second-round knockout.

Any thoughts of Bruno being taken into the later rounds in this bout scheduled for ten evaporated very quickly. Evans was well and truly out of his depth, floundering in deep water without a lifeguard on hand when Bruno found the punch score a knockout and end his opponent's contribution to the fight in round two. Evans had been on the back foot from the start, and took a count before the bell sounded to end the first round. The American was down again for a second time in the second stanza, beating the count only to walk into a Bruno left hook moments later. This really was not a bad performance from the home fighter, whose spiteful punching power was a most valuable asset for him and not one to be underestimated by his opponents.

This was the last time that Evans suffered a defeat in the professional ring. After the Bruno bout, he went on to win his next eight fights, which included winning the lightly regarded vacant Global Federation world heavyweight crown on 1 June 2002 by knocking out Allen Smith in round four. Evans had his last professional bout on 2 February 2003, stopping Jeff Lally in round four.

Oliver McCall

On 24 September 1994, American Oliver McCall proved to be a big parcel full of surprises when he did the unexpected in his challenge for the WBC world heavyweight title held by Lennox Lewis. The American caused a sensation when, against all expectations, he stopped the champion in two rounds. This opened the door for Bruno to challenge once again for the championship.

After defeating Lewis, McCall made one successful defence of the championship against former WBC and IBF title holder Larry Homes, outpointing him over twelve rounds on 8 April 1995. While Holmes was just a shadow of the fighter he had once been, he was still a top-level operator with a great deal of pride and experience behind him. Calling on all his know-how, Holmes gave McCall a testing night. However, the champion pressed his challenger and would not be denied; he looked a worthy holder of the title, picking his punches well to retain the crown.

Bruno and McCall met on 2 September 1995 at Wembley Stadium in a fight tagged 'The Empire Strikes Back'. The American entered the ring with a record of twenty-six wins in thirty-one bouts, eighteen of them coming inside the distance. There was no doubt that Bruno was in the last-chance saloon. It was clearly his last role of the dice: if he lost in this bid for the title, it would surely be the end of his world championship hopes. This time, the fat lady had reached the last verse of her song—there would be no encore.

Indeed, a fourth chance for Bruno to win the world title was something many had not realistically expected to happen after his failures against Tim Witherspoon, Mike Tyson, and Lennox Lewis. It was rare for a challenger to be given four chances at the title after having suffered losses in his previous attempts. However, there was a precedent for such an event set by American Jersey Joe Walcott, who succeeded in his fifth attempt at the championship after previous challenges ended in failure. Walcott's first chance at the championship came on 5 December 1947 against title holder Joe Louis, who retained the title on points after fifteen rounds. Walcott stepped in with Louis for a second time on 25 June 1948 and was knocked out in round eleven. When Louis retired from the sport, Walcott met Ezzard Charles for the vacant NBA version of the title, and once again the title eluded him when he was outpointed after fifteen rounds on 22 June 1949. On 7 March 1951, Walcott had another crack at Charles, who had become the undisputed king of the division. Once again, he was on the wrong side of a fifteen-round points decision. Jersey Joe was handed yet another title tilt on 18 July 1951 against Charles, and while many may have felt the win was a formality for the defending title holder, Walcott amazingly struck gold dust when he knocked out the champion in round seven.

The task ahead was not an easy one for Bruno; McCall epitomised what a ring-smart professional was all about. The man had every intention of making his second defence a winning one. It may well have resonated in McCall's mind that every time Bruno stepped up to challenge for a world crown he finished in second place, for which there were no prizes. Therefore, confidence for McCall in this contest was not in short supply, because of the belief that this would be a routine defence, one in which he would emulate Tim Witherspoon, Mike Tyson, and Lennox Lewis in turning back the Bruno challenge. By the end of the contest, he believed he would emerge the victor by a late stoppage or knockout, and thus take his title back to the USA.

When the bout started, Bruno went about his work with a good, effective left jab—chants of 'Bruno, Bruno' ringing out from all corners of the arena from the spectators offering him every encouragement. Bruno took early control, scoring with hurtful punches and keeping his opponent off balance. McCall appeared to have trouble getting his own punches off in the early stages, but he always looked dangerous. Throughout the contest, Bruno kept a high level of concentration, boxing an intelligent fight and having to absorb a few hard blows along the way, although it was encouraging to see that he took them without any ill effect. Bruno was doing well, of that there was no doubt, but one could not help but have a sense of foreboding, for he was also doing well in previous bouts with James Smith, Tim Witherspoon, and Lennox Lewis before his opponents thus found the punch to end matters. It was hoped that a repeat of those past encounters would not take place on this night. It was a strain for many of the Bruno fans who were watching the contest, resulting in sweaty palms and heart rates that were escalating by the second. There was the constant fear that Bruno might run out of steam and walk onto one of McCall's big punches.

It is surprising how agonisingly long a three-minute round can be in the heat of battle. Bruno dug in and fought the fight of his life in what only can be described as a gargantuan effort to snatch the crown. Both men took their share of punches as the rounds rolled on, but then, as the saying goes, you cannot take a shower without getting wet.

The championship was within touching distance. Bruno was so near his goal. He had boxed his way into a lead, which was good. However, the respective points he had garnered could be wiped out and rendered negligible if McCall landed solidly on Bruno's whiskers with one of his ever-threatening right hooks. Bruno had to take care, not switch off, and ensure that he was not caught by the kind of punch that put paid to Lewis when he had lost the crown to McCall. It was obvious that the American was still very much in the fight. It would have been cruel had Bruno run out of steam and failed in what was his finest moment.

The fight was intense. It had all the drama of a *Rocky* picture, but this was no movie. This was the real thing—real blood, real sweat, and real pain, all without the attraction of stirring music in the background. Bruno eventually started to show signs of exhaustion. During the battle, his stamina and will were tested like never before. If Bruno wanted the title, he had to dig deep and draw on any reserves he had left in the energy bank, which must have been running dangerously low. Bruno had yet to travel twelve rounds in a contest, while McCall had completed that distance twice. This was a fact that could prove to be a crucial and deciding factor in the fight, one that would favour the champion with the experience of coping with the extra rounds both mentally and physically. Could Bruno actually win the crown in his fourth and ultimately final attempt? Or was the possibility too much to expect?

The partisan crowd got behind Bruno and cheered their man on to what they hoped would prove to be his best victory in the paid ranks—one that would bring him the ultimate prize. In the last round McCall went for broke, attempting to land the telling punch that would finish the contest and see him retain the title. These were anxious moments for the challenger. Bruno now looked a spent force, but thankfully he kept it together and held on until the final bell rang out to signal that the bout was over. At the end of twelve pulsating rounds, a new world heavyweight champion was crowned. Bruno was awarded a well-deserved points victory, much to the jubilation of his fans in attendance on this very special night.

The ring was invaded by a group of well-wishers, which included the reigning WBC world super-middleweight king Nigel Benn, and WBC International super-bantamweight champion 'Prince' Naseem Hamed. A firework display and the falling of ticker tape inside the arena added to the excitement of the night.

Both warriors gave their best, laying everything on the line. McCall had had the greatest moment in his boxing career when he won his world crown in Britain, and clearly he had his worst when he lost it there. This was, without exception, Bruno's *tour de force* moment. Bruno, having being written off by many, was the WBC heavyweight champion of the world. It had taken Bruno thirteen years, five months, and sixteen days to capture the crown, which at times looked to be well out of his reach.

It was an uplifting moment for a man who just would not give up, and had, in a way, been an inspiration for many who had met with setbacks in their lives and careers. Standing in the ring, the WBC championship belt strapped securely to his waist, the criticism Bruno had taken for the quality of his opponents in the early stages of his career seemed light years away. It was a fantastic moment for Bruno, his many fans, and British Boxing. It was a night to savour and enjoy.

Bruno had achieved his ambition at the fourth attempt and in so doing had deservedly earned the admiration and respect of those in and outside the world of boxing for his courage, spirit, and firm belief that he would one day be a world heavyweight champion. While Terry Lawless was no longer Bruno's manager, there was no doubt that he would have been more than delighted that his former charge had at long last won the championship he so desired.

Mike Tyson (II)

After all the deserved publicity, fuss, and attention in the months that followed, it was time for Bruno to go back to the serious side of his profession and put the championship on the line. It was a case of 'after the sweet, expect the bitter', since everything comes at a cost and the cost of winning the world heavyweight crown was high—it came in the form of having to meet Mike Tyson for the second time.

The American was set to be Bruno's first challenger for the championship, and the outing looked to be very bitter for the British world title holder. Bruno's defence of the WBC crown was not going to be easy or an enviable one, not by a long shot. Even casual followers of the sport were aware of this fact. Bruno's chances of keeping the crown did not look good and there was no getting past this fact. Bruno had achieved his dream of winning the world title and now he faced what looked like a nightmare defence.

Since their first meeting on 25 February 1989, in which Bruno suffered a five-round stoppage defeat, Tyson had lost his undefeated record, along with his world championship, when knocked out in round ten on 11 February 1990 by fellow American James Douglas. Tyson also had to deal with various well-documented problems outside the ring to compound his woes. Despite all this, Tyson was a fearsome fighter who could not be dismissed out of hand. He had won his last six bouts in a row since his defeat to Douglas and had complied a record of forty-three wins with just one defeat.

Bruno would engage his challenger at the MGM Grand in Las Vegas. Many were of the opinion that Bruno's first defence would be his last and he would thus leave America with one less item than he entered the country with—that item being his championship belt. There were some who held the optimistic view that Bruno just might surprise Tyson, who was not the fighter he once was, but this was only a small glimmer of hope that had no real substance. Sad to say, from a British boxing point of view, pundits who knew the fight game and did not look at the encounter with rose-tinted glasses firmly tipped Tyson to punch his way back to the title.

On 16 March 1996, the expectations of those who feared the worst for the British fighter proved to true, when Tyson regained the crown by stopping Bruno in round three. For the second time, the American proved too powerful. From the very first seconds of round one, Tyson attacked perennially, catching Bruno with solid, hurtful punches. Tyson hit the Briton with the kind of power and force that most men on the safe side of the ropes would not be able to stand up to—indeed, they would need hospital treatment urgently had they been on the receiving end of said blows. The American was still able to bring a considerable amount of heat into the ring, any signs of deterioration in his form certainly did not manifest itself in this contest. Tyson was on fire and Bruno was getting badly burned, with no way to extinguish the flames engulfing him. Bruno ended the first session with a badly cut left eye caused by a right hand that Tyson had landed. Having such an injury so early in the bout was a massive set-back for Bruno. Like so many other fighters before him, Bruno could not turn back the ever-advancing fighting machine in front of him. In the second stanza, the head and body of Bruno continued to take a series of solid blows that both bruised and bloodied the flesh. This round was not a good one for Bruno since he was docked a point for constant holding by the referee. Bruno did his best during the bout, but he always came in a very poor second to Tyson in a contest that at no point looked like lasting the full twelve rounds.

This proved to be Bruno's last professional contest. It was sad to see Bruno exit the sport this way, but, at the end of the day, his last bout was a world championship fight. While he did not end on a winning note, he did bow out with a high profile contest.

Bruno retired from the sport with a respectable record of forty wins (thirty-eight inside the distance by a knockout or stoppage) in forty-five bouts, winning the WBC world heavyweight title and the European crown along the way.

Bruno did not challenge for the British or Commonwealth championship during his career, which in some respects was a shame since he would not only have won both of these the titles, but when considering the boxers in action in the UK at that time would surely have won the Lonsdale Belt outright for making two successful defences of the domestic crown. Clearly, the management team behind Bruno had their own clear plan of action that could not be faulted since it proved to be a successful one. Bruno may not have been a world champion for long, but it is better to be a king for a day than not at all. Bruno was only defeated by men who were or went on to win a version of the world championship: James Smith, Tim Witherspoon, Mike Tyson (twice), and Lennox Lewis.

Bruno was also honoured by being awarded an MBE. Bruno was a credit to boxing and always gave of his best; he never short-changed his fans. Bruno will always be remembered with great affection by those who followed the sport—especially his banter and friendship with the highly-respected sports commentator Harry Carpenter. It was great to hear the big man asking when interviewed, 'where's 'Arry?' They were a great double act.

2

Lennox Lewis

It is often said that 'all that glitters is not gold'. Well, we all know from experience how true that saying is. Nonetheless, in the case of Lennox Lewis nothing could have been further from the truth—in fact, it was the complete opposite.

Lewis, who was born on 2 September 1965 in West Ham, London, was a man destined from the start to have a golden future in boxing. However, his boxing talent was almost lost to Britain when his family decided to emigrate to Canada in a bid to start a new life. In his newly adopted country, Lewis excelled at various sports, including boxing. It was clear to those that knew the game that Lewis had the ability to make an impression in the square ring should he concentrate his efforts in that direction.

Lewis started to live up to said expectations in the years that followed with some impressive performances. He fought his way to various honours in the unpaid ranks, which included winning a gold medal for Canada at super-heavyweight in the 1986 Commonwealth Games in Edinburgh, Scotland. On this occasion, Lewis became the first man to win gold at this newly introduced weight division at this event. This was followed by further success when winning gold at the 1988 Olympic Games in Seoul, South Korea, by stopping future professional world heavyweight champion Riddick Bowe of America in two rounds in the super-heavyweight final. When Lewis decided to punch for pay, he returned to Britain under the guidance of manager Frank Maloney. With such an outstanding pedigree in the amateur ranks, Lewis, who stood at 6 feet and 5 inches, was deemed to have a bright future ahead of him—he would clearly be under the microscope and scrutinised at every turn when plying his trade. Lewis would be a most welcome addition to the ranks of British boxing, which at the time was still waiting for a home fighter to capture the world heavyweight crown. So, even before he had thrown the first punch in the paid ranks, like Frank Bruno he would have a great deal of pressure resting on his shoulders.

Al Malcolm

Lewis entered the professional ranks on 27 June 1989 to face the then reigning Midlands Area heavyweight champion Al Malcolm. Hailing from Birmingham, Malcolm was an experienced boxer and on record looked a decent enough opponent for Lewis's maiden paid fight.

The British champion at the time was Gary Mason who, on his professional debut, had also met Malcolm in a contest that had taken place on 16 October 1984, defeating him by a knockout in round one. The pair met in a return bout on 14 December 1984 when Mason once again triumphed when the referee stopped the bout in round two.

During his time in the ring, the Brummie had won eleven of his previous twenty-four bouts, with one draw. While the most obvious outcome of the contest was a victory for Lewis inside the distance, it did appear that Malcolm would last a few rounds against the new prospect before facing the exit door. The fans expected much of Lewis and he did not disappoint, quickly stamping his authority on the contest scheduled for six rounds. The bout, which took place at the Royal Albert Hall, witnessed Lewis piling on the pressure from the outset, landing hard blows to both head and body. At times he looked a little wild in his attacks, leaving himself open to counters that his opponent might throw back. However, it had to be taken into consideration that this was his first outing in the punch-for-pay ranks and he was obviously keen to impress. Any faults in the fighting style of Lewis would be ironed out with experience in the fullness of time. Lewis continued to attack and landed a left hook, which landed flush on Malcolm's jaw, sending him down to the canvas for a count in round one. It looked for a moment as if Lewis was going to score a first-round victory in his debut, which would have been an excellent start, but it was not to be. Malcolm managed to get to his feet and survived until the second stanza, whereupon his interest in the bout concluded courtesy of the hard-hitting Lewis landing the finishing blow that saw him duly counted out. Lewis had started his journey in the paid ranks in a most impressive manner one that promised much for his future.

The following night, Gary Mason successfully defended his British heavyweight crown against challenger Jess Harding at the International

Centre at Brentwood in Essex, winning with a second-round stoppage—Mason and Lewis were destined to meet in the future.

Bruce Johnson

Lewis's second bout took him away from the British Isles to the USA and the Convention Centre in Atlantic City on 21 July 1989 against the home-grown Bruce Johnson. A prospect will often have indulged in a number of bouts on their own ground before undertaking such a venture abroad—especially to the USA. This showed the massive confidence that the team had in the ability of Lewis. If the match was construed as a calculated risk, then it was a good one; Lewis proved too much for his opponent, and proceedings ended when the referee stepped in to stop the contest in round two.

Johnson, with a record of sixteen bouts, winning five, losing ten, and drawing one, was not a top-notch fighter—that much was obvious even to a non-follower of the sport. However, the American looked confident enough, and had the slight advantage of fighting in his own country against an opponent who had only participated in one paid bout. The lack of professional know-how did not hamper Lewis. Once the bell sounded to start the six-round contest, it was apparent that the American had little chance of upsetting the British fighter—it was one-way traffic and Lewis was doing all the driving. He won without being pushed too hard. As always in a match of this nature, the experience of fighting in the States was a rewarding factor regardless of the calibre of the opponent. It was necessary to get the feel of boxing in the country where all the top heavyweights, both past and present, came from. If all went to plan for Lewis, big bouts in the USA would be forthcoming. It was interesting to note that one of Johnson's prior defeats came against future WBC world heavyweight champion Oliver McCall on 1 October 1988, a fighter who knocked him out promptly in round one.

Andrew Gerrard

It was back to the UK for Lewis to take on Andrew Gerrard on 25 September 1989 at the National Sports Centre in Crystal Palace, London. Gerrard had comprised a tally of forty-seven bouts, winning eleven, losing thirty, and drawing five, with one no contest. The win ratio of Gerrard was not one that inspired confidence in his chances of obtaining a victory over Lewis. Gerrard was not going to give Lewis any grey hairs, or indeed cause him to have any sleepless nights. The Welshman was, however, a fighter who always gave his all and would not give up easily if there was any chance at all of a win—he would take it, for that is what fighters do. Gerrard was totally aware that an upset victory over Lewis would do his career no harm whatsoever. In his last bout before crossing gloves with Lewis, Gerrard had lost in his challenge for the Welsh Area heavyweight crown, losing a ten-round points decision to holder Chris Jacobs on 8 June 1989.

From the start of the contest, Lewis found his man with stinging jabs to the head mixed with heavy shots that he sunk into his torso. As the rounds passed by, Gerrard continued to ship punishment from Lewis, but stubbornly stood up to the rain of punches that frequently found their targets on his body. There was no surrender in Gerrard who defiantly stood his ground, but it was clear that the sands of time were running out for him in the bout. Lewis landed his punches at will, with little or no threatening blows coming back at him from his brave opponent. Lewis was taken into the fourth round of a contest set for six whereupon he gained victory when the referee halted the bout in his favour. Lewis looked comfortable during the contest and, as expected, had at no time been in danger of losing his undefeated record to Gerrard. Lewis was clearly a league above the Welshman in every department of boxing.

Steve Garber

Steve Garber stepped to do battle with Lewis on 10 October 1989 at the City Hall in Hull, Yorkshire. Garber had put together a record of thirteen wins, ten defeats, and one draw. There was no skirting around the fact that Lewis was once again expected to win, and this he did in fine style. In fact, the fans did not see much of Lewis in the contest that was scheduled for six rounds since he brought down the curtain with a knockout in the opening stanza. Lewis showed he had punching power to go with his undoubted boxing skills.

While Lewis was obviously a great boost for UK boxing, it was not all plain sailing since he had two battles to overcome when he stepped into the ring. While his opponent was the first obstacle, the second, and perhaps the most difficult of all, were the British public, who he had yet to gain acceptance from. Many felt at the time that Lewis, despite being born in Britain, was at heart a Canadian, since he had spent his younger years in the country and had thus won a number of amateur honours along with his Olympic gold medal under the flag with the maple leaf and was, to some extent, using the

UK as a convenient route to the top. However, in the fullness of time Lewis won over the many fans who supported him, and hence became proud of his vast achievements inside the square ring.

Melvin Epps

On 5 November 1989, American fighter Melvin Epps gloved up to take on Lewis at the Royal Albert Hall. The contest was cast for the duration of six rounds. Epps was a very experienced fighter, having fought on thirty-four occasions, winning fourteen bouts, losing nineteen, and drawing one. The record was not too impressive, but the boxer from the USA was not a man to be viewed as an easy night's work. Epps was also no stranger to UK shores, having previously crossed the Atlantic to outpoint former British heavyweight champion Hughroy Currie over eight rounds on 3 December 1986 at the Alexandra Pavilion in Muswell Hill, London. Epps showed in his victory over Currie that he was a tricky operator. Nonetheless, Epps was not so successful on British soil during this outing, having been disqualified in round two for not obeying the referee's instructions. Epps was not happy about the decision—one that many of the spectators in attendance booed. The contest proved to be a bad-tempered affair that sadly failed to get going and, despite the date, failed to produce any fireworks. Therefore, Lewis was unable to display any sparkle or produce magic in the ring on this outing.

Greg Gorrell

Lewis had his sixth contest of the year on 18 December 1989 at the Memorial Auditorium in Kitchener, Ontario, Canada. The opposition was Greg Gorrell from the USA, who was halted in the fifth of an eight-round contest. Prior to meeting Lewis, the only name of note on Gorrell's slate was French fighter Anaclet Wamba, who fought the American and stopped him in the first round on 23 April 1988. Wamba, however, was not a true heavyweight. He was a cruiserweight—the weight division below and where he gained the most success during his career. This fact was confirmed when he went on to capture the European cruiserweight crown on 11 November 1989 by outpointing defending champion Angelo Rottoli of Italy over twelve rounds. On 20 July 1991, he then won the WBC world cruiserweight title stopping holder Massimiliano Duran also from Italy in round eleven.

Gorrell, who boxed in the southpaw stance, entered the ring against Lewis with a record of twenty-one wins and seven defeats. Lewis started the contest quickly, throwing various combinations at his opponent and scoring a knockdown in the opening round with a solid right, that landed flush on target. Gorrell looked shaky and took a compulsory count of eight from the referee before being allowed to continue. At that moment in time, it looked as if the American fighter would be lucky to survive in to the second round as he looked ready for the taking. However, Gorrell showed a fighter's heart, carrying on rather than looking for the easy way out. Gorrell hoped that he might somehow find a way through Lewis's defence and connect with punishing blows of his own to upset the odds. The American tried to make a competitive fight against Lewis, but he was hopelessly outclassed, and thus unable to contain the undefeated British fighter, who was always one step ahead of him. During the bout, Lewis was in full flow and put together a series of classy jabs mixed with solid blows to overcome his opponent and, in so, doing further confirm his potential.

Noel Quarless

Lewis was soon back in action in 1990, eager to continue his climb upwards in the domestic rankings. Lewis's seventh opponent on 31 January was Noel Quarless from Liverpool. Quarless was no easy pickings as he was something of a danger man. His record of nineteen wins and eleven defeats was not overly impressive at first sight, but it was undeniable that he had some punching power in his mitts, having stopped or knocked out eleven of his opponents. To his credit, he had defeated some good fighters along the way, men like former WBA world heavyweight champion John Tate from the USA, who he had outpointed over ten rounds on 30 March 1988 in what was an excellent performance, considering the American had won his last fourteen bouts in a row. While his prime was behind him, he had still been considered a level above the British fighter, and had not come to the UK as a fall guy. The American had been looking to add another win to his CV, but was surprised by the somewhat unheralded Brit.

Quarless had also surprised many other fighters who had been favoured over him when they entered the ring to do battle against him. Quarless provided a shock on 13 October 1983 against Sweden's future two-time European heavyweight champion, Anders Eklund, who he stopped in the first round. The man from Liverpool also shocked again when he stopped former British, European, and Commonwealth heavyweight king John. L. Gardner in round two on 2 November 1983.

Quarless's performance in the ring blew hot and cold: nobody ever knew which version of the fighter would turn up. Nonetheless, one thing was certain: he was an opponent that could not be written off—if Quarless was up for it, he had the ability to make life most uncomfortable for Lewis. Quarless was no respecter for reputation; he would fight any boxer put in front of him at any time. Therefore, the danger signs were there for Lewis that the opponent he was facing was more than capable of producing an upset on the night if the opportunity presented itself. One way or another, the contest did not look like it would go the full six rounds. It appeared that Lewis just might have a testing time and run into trouble should he get careless and Quarless find his chin with one of his damaging punches. Quarless was entering the ring to face Lewis with two consecutive victories behind him and was hoping to add Lewis to that list and make it three.

Once again, Lewis showed his class. He brought his vast array of skills into play at York Hall in Bethnal Green, London, to close the show without too much effort to stop his man in round two. The man from Liverpool did have a brief moment of success in the first session when he landed a solid right on Lewis's chin. Where such a blow might have put a lesser man in trouble and put him in defensive mode, Lewis showed no ill effects from the punch. This must have been a little discouraging for Quarless as well as confirmation to any doubters, if there were any at the time, that Lewis had the durability (at least at this level) to take a punch. In the second round Lewis went up a gear and looked for the finish, unloading a series of punches on his foe. Quarless was not able to stand up to the power of Lewis's blows and was down twice in round two—the second knockdown prompting the referee to step in and stop the contest, saving him from taking further punishment. Quarless appeared one-dimensional during the course of the contest while Lewis showed a great deal of variety in his work. It became abundantly clear moments after the bell had sounded to start the battle that Quarless was not going to be the man to hinder Lewis's ascension in the heavyweight ranks.

Calvin Jones

American Calvin Jones was the next fighter to enter the square ring against Lewis on 22 March 1990 at the Leisure Centre, Gateshead, Tyne and Wear. Jones had a record of 13 wins and 4 defeats. Three of the fighters who had defeated him were quality men like former WBA world heavyweight champion John Tate, who had outpointed him over four rounds on 28 November 1987. James Smith, another former holder of the WBA world heavyweight crown, who had shared the ring with Jones and thus stopped him in eight rounds on 29 September 1989. Jones later stepped in to do battle with former IBF world heavyweight champion Tony Tucker on 8 January 1990 and found himself once again in the loser's column when his opponent found the punch to knock him out in round five.

It could be thought, with some justification, that after sharing the ring with boxers of that ilk, he would be able to push Lewis a little and take him into the later rounds and make him work a little for his win, thus giving him a few problems to overcome. The Briton, despite his impressive amateur pedigree, was a novice in professional terms, with just seven bouts behind him. Therefore, the contest set for eight rounds looked promising—yet Lewis stopped Jones impressively by knockout in the first round.

Michael Simuwelu

Zambian Michael Simuwelu was the next to step up to the plate, meeting Lewis at the Royal Albert Hall on 14 April 1990. Simuwelu came armed with a record that consisted of eighteen wins, two defeats, and one draw. His CV suggested that Simuwelu might make Lewis dig in a little to achieve a victory in this contest, but any such prediction was way off base. The fight, which was slated for eight rounds, was a one-horse race that came to a close when Lewis stopped Simuwelu in the first round with a well-timed left hook that landed on target. It was obvious that Simuwelu had no other plan to fall back on once Lewis started to leather him.

Such bouts were proving that, even at this early stage of his paid boxing career, Lewis was ready for better opposition. A slight step up to meet better fighters was now warranted—not world class, of course, but more durable foes who would not say goodnight so quickly after being hit. Some trees fall in the middle of a storm, while others bend and remain firm, surviving the force. The British fighter needed opponents who would not fall so easily but survive the storm that he generated inside the ring.

As always when bringing along a young hopeful though, caution had to be the order of the day to ensure that there were no nasty shocks waiting for him along the way. Taking the right fight at the right time is vital; put a fighter in with an opponent who bales out too quickly and the critics come out in forceful condemnation about the weakness of the opposition. Match a fighter with an opponent much better than expected that leaves the young hopeful defeated, then the critics come out in force once again, only this time singing a different tune, bemoaning the fact that the up-and-coming fighter was foolishly put in too soon against quality opposition. It really is a case of not being able to win whichever way. While Lewis was without doubt a shining star among the crop of heavyweight hopefuls, he still had to be handled cautiously to garner experience, which was vital before he stepped in with the big guns of the division.

Jorge Alfredo Dascola

Lewis entered the Royal Albert Hall once again on 9 May 1990 to do battle with Jorge Alfredo Dascola from Argentina. With a record of fourteen wins and three defeats, Dascola looked like a man who could give Lewis a real argument and a few problems to overcome—possibly taking him the full eight-round distance, which would be a good learning experience.

In his last contest on 5 February 1990 at the Great Western Forum in Inglewood, California, Dascola had fought former WBA world heavyweight king Michael Dokes for the WBA Inter-Continental heavyweight title. While he had been stopped in round eleven, he had still been able to extend the American. The golden days of Dokes may have been a distant memory, but he was still a capable performer, so this was a good effort by Dascola.

However, if fans had expected to see a competitive match against Lewis, they were disappointed when Dascola was counted out in the first round.

Dan Murphy

On 20 May 1990, American Dan Murphy was the next to face Lewis and hopefully test him a little more sternly. The contest was set for eight rounds. The big question now was whether Murphy would be yet another opponent to say goodnight inside the first round.

The bout took place at the City Hall in Sheffield, Yorkshire. Murphy's record of twenty-five wins, four defeats, and one draw looked impressive, but there was one result that set alarm bells ringing—a fighter by the name of Michael Simuwelu had knocked Murphy out in one round on 10 October 1986. This was the very same fighter who Lewis had dispatched in the first round on 14 April 1990. Based on that result, another very early night looked to be on the cards once again for Lewis.

It did not take long after the first bell sounded to realise that Lewis was the superior fighter. Lewis was aggressive from the off, looking for the pay-off punch. As duly expected, he won yet again inside the distance, but not as quickly as first thought by many pundits. Murphy proved to be resilient, surprisingly hanging in there with the British fighter even though he took some solid licks for his pains during the bout. He finished with a damaged nose that was bleeding badly. Lewis had to work a little harder in this contest since he had to travel to round six to secure his stoppage win. Murphy proved a very elusive target, moving quickly around the ring and making Lewis chase him to land his shots. The American was defensively minded and not keen to engage Lewis, who carried the more hurtful punches in his armoury. This was the furthest that Lewis had fought to date since joining the paid ranks, which was not a bad thing, since it would prove beneficial to the Britons' ring experience. First-round victories look great on the record for the victorious fighter, but in truth do very little to add to his boxing acumen.

Ossie Ocasio

In his next bout, Lewis did indeed step up a level, by meeting former world champion Ossie Ocasio at the Royal Albert Hall. This was a good pairing, a clever and sensible match that the British fighter was more than capable of winning, and one in which he could gain vital experience against a slick opponent who knew the many tricks of the trade.

Puerto Rican-born Ocasio, who had the nickname 'Jaws', was a boxer who had previously held the WBA world cruiserweight crown, winning the vacant championship on 13 February 1982 by outpointing Robbie Williams over fifteen rounds. Ocasio lost said crown in his fourth defence on 1 December 1984 to Piet Crous by way of a fifteen-round points decision. The Puerto Rican fighter had shared the ring with a staggering number of top fighters during his career, men like Jimmy Young, who he had outpointed over ten rounds on 9 June 1978 and 27 January 1979. Ocasio also met future WBA world heavyweight king Michael Dokes twice: firstly on 19 April 1980, which resulted in a ten-round draw; then on 28 June 1980 in a return bout in which Ocasio did not fair quite so well, suffering a first-round stoppage. Ocasio then captured a ten-round points decision over former WBA world cruiserweight title holder Dwight Muhammad Qawi on 15 May 1987. A later attempt to regain the cruiserweight crown on 15 August 1987 from the then reigning WBA and IBF champion Evander Holyfield ended in failure when he was stopped in round eleven. Further defeats followed at the hands of future WBO world heavyweight champion Ray Mercer, who outpointed him over eight rounds on 7 December 1989. Tyrell Biggs then won a ten-round points decision over him on 11 January 1990. Future WBA world heavyweight king Bruce Seldon proved too ring savvy and won an eight-round points decision on 18 May 1990.

The pinnacle of Ocasio's ring career, apart from holding the WBA world cruiserweight title, was his shot at the WBC world heavyweight crown on 23 March 1979, in just his fourteenth professional contest, against the much more experienced holder Larry Holmes. The challenge ended in defeat for Ocasio, who was very much the underdog for the fight. Holmes thus knew too much for his opponent and stopped him in the seventh round.

Ocasio was no stranger to the British Isles, since he had previously fought in the UK at Wembley Arena on 17 March 1981—a visit that did not hold happy memories for him. Ocasio had been matched with John L. Gardner, the former British, European, and Commonwealth heavyweight champion, and crashed to defeat when knocked out in round six.

Prior to meeting Lewis, Ocasio had accumulated a record of thirty-two bouts, winning twenty-two, losing nine, and drawing one. On 27 June 1990, Lewis went the full distance for the first time when he showed that he was able to box the extra rounds when called upon to do so. Lewis was unable to emulate fellow Briton John L. Gardner and stop his man, but he looked comfortable in outpointing Ocasio over eight rounds. Lewis was too lively for his opponent, out-thinking and outmanoeuvring the Puerto Rican fighter throughout the duration of the contest. This was a good result and it also added a little glitter to his record, since having a victory over a former champion of the world does not do an up-and-coming fighter any harm. In fact, it adds a little kudos to his name.

Ocasio returned to the UK on 3 October 1990 to meet another Briton, Jess Harding, in a ten-round contest. This visit proved to be third time lucky after the defeats he had suffered against Lewis and Gardner. At the Festival Hall in Basildon, Essex, Ocasio won his first contest on UK soil when Harding retired in round eight.

Mike Acey

Lewis paid a second professional visit to Canada, his formerly adopted country, on 11 July 1990 to face American opponent Mike Acey at the Superstars Nite Club in Kitchener, Ontario. Acey, with a record of sixteen fights, winning eleven, losing four, and drawing one, was not going to shock the Briton. In fact, he was practically made to order for Lewis. The contest was scheduled for ten rounds, but there was little chance that the bout would last that long. This did not make it a bad match, however, since Acey had fought Riddick Bowe on 19 October 1989 where he was stopped in the opening round. The thinking was that if Acey was worthy enough to step in with the highly regarded Bowe, then he had to be a suitable foe for Lewis, irrespective of his quick defeat to the American. Lewis took a little longer than Bowe to send his man back to the dressing room, delivering the *coup de grâce* by knocking out Acey in round two.

It was not an epic affair—few, if any, expected it to be so. Once the bell sounded to start the fight, it was clear that a three-legged horse at the Grand National would have had a better chance of romping home to victory than Acey had of hearing the final bell. The American was down for a count twice in the first round and twice in the second. On the first knockdown in the second stanza, Lewis was admonished by the referee for letting his punches go when his opponent was on the canvas. This action brought a chorus of boos from various spectators around the ring. Once the bout continued, Lewis continued to attack Acey, who was now ready for the taking. Ultimately, it was a damaging body punch, landed with sickening force , which brought the bout to a close. It was not a fight that would further enhance Lewis's ring education, but it was a bout that kept Lewis busy while waiting for more meaningful bouts in the pipeline.

Jean-Maurice Chanet

Lewis's team were now confident that it was time for their boxer to take a vital leap to another level. This he did when he made his first bid for a major title: the European heavyweight crown, held by Jean-Maurice Chanet of France. The European title is a good championship to own since, as the name implies, the holder is the champion of a great deal of territory—and of course gives international recognition, status, and a lift upwards in the world rankings.

Chanet had taken the crown from Britain's Derek Williams on 3 February 1990 by way of a twelve-round points decision, and had repeated the twelve-round points win in a return contest on 28 May 1990. Both bouts had taken place in France, so Chanet had had home ground advantage in the two battles with Williams.

Chanet had fought in the UK once before, when he dropped an eight-round points decision to domestic fighter Jess Harding on 16 December 1988 at the International Centre in Brentwood, Essex. The Frenchman had a record of twenty-four wins and ten defeats. Chanet was a competent fighter but, when considering their respective form, a Lewis victory was expected.

At the National Sports Centre in Crystal Palace, on 31 October 1990, Lewis put in a good performance, dominating the champion from the off. The contest was not a thrill-a-minute affair. The British challenger picked his punches and landed with precision to both the head and body. The gulf in class showed as the rounds progressed—the title changed hands when Chanet, badly cut over the left eye, was halted in the sixth round to give the Briton his predicted win. While the cut was the cause of the stoppage, there was no doubt that Lewis was headed for victory with or without it. The Frenchman was game, but at no time did he look a likely winner against Lewis in what was a very one-sided contest. On winning the championship, Lewis became the eleventh fighter from the UK to claim the crown since the International Boxing Union became the European Boxing Union in 1946. The previous British holders were Bruce Woodcock, Jack Gardner, Dick Richardson, Henry Cooper (three times), Joe Bugner (three times), Jack Bodell, Richard Dunn, John L. Gardner, Frank Bruno and Derek Williams.

The victory somewhat elevated Lewis into the mainstream of heavyweight boxing, confirming that he was a fighter at the weight to take seriously. However, despite the win over Chanet, the victory had to be viewed realistically. The win was by no means a barometer on how Lewis would fair against a rated fighter. Chanet was not a world-ranked heavyweight, and the win over the Frenchman was not likely to send the top contenders running for cover. There were many tougher and more talented men in the division than Chanet, the like of which Lewis had yet to meet. Tasting the punches of higher-echelon fighters and shaking them off was a far different ball game altogether, and that would be the superior test for Lewis when that time eventually came. The path towards the summit was littered with hopefuls who could not make the grade when put to the sword. It was vital for fans not to get too carried away at this stage and put the victory in perspective, thus allowing Lewis to climb the division's ladder with intelligent and educational bouts. The need to rush and meet top, world-ranked contenders had to be tempered until the moment was right. Up to this point in time, the team behind Lewis had been making all the right choices for their fighter, of that there was no doubt.

Gary Mason

Next up was a more demanding fight for Lewis, one in which some experts felt he could come unstuck. The man he was to face was the reigning British heavyweight champion, Gary Mason, a fighter who would not submit easily. Mason was undefeated in thirty-five fights and world ranked. Mason had world title ambitions of his own and would fight hard to keep his crown and ranking.

Mason had bested men like former WBC world cruiserweight champion Alfonzo Ratliff, who he stopped in six rounds on 3 February 1988; and another former world cruiserweight king (IBF version) Ricky Parkey had tasted defeated at the Briton's hands when he was stopped in round one on 9 March 1988. James Tillis was stopped in round five on 30 November 1988, and Tyrell Biggs was knocked out in round seven on 4 October 1989. Mason had won the vacant British heavyweight crown on 18 January 1989 by knocking out former title holder Hughroy Currie in round four. Mason had made his first successful defence against Jess Harding on 28 June 1989 with a second-round stoppage. So, it could be said with confidence that Mason was a far better and more dangerous opponent than Lewis's last victim, Jean-Maurice Chanet. In fact, had Mason fought Chanet, he too would have been the favourite to have his arm lifted in victory once the proceedings were over. Mason was not in the ring to give Lewis an easy ride or to make him look good or help enhance his reputation in any way—he was there to win, and win big. This was an exciting pairing between two men who were looking to advance beyond British and European honours. There was no doubting whatsoever that this was Lewis's toughest opponent since turning to the paid ranks: for the British champion, a great deal was riding on this contest. A victory over Lewis would see him win the Lonsdale belt outright, a prize that he, like most other domestic champions both past and present, wanted to keep. The contest set for twelve rounds was a double title fight with both Mason's British and Lewis's European titles on the line.

As expected, on 6 March 1991 at the Wembley Arena, Mason gave Lewis a hard night. He looked capable of pushing Lewis the full distance, but the ex-Olympic champion came through to stop his man in round seven and thus add the British title to his name. Mason was a good fighter, and a worthy holder of the domestic championship, but Lewis was much sharper and faster, delivering the more accurate and damaging blows. Mason showed the signs of battle, finishing the bout with his right eye closed and an additional cut over his left. This was Lewis's best win to date. He was moving up the rankings and it now looked at this stage of his career that only a top-rated fighter could give him trouble.

Mike Weaver

The next outing took place on 12 July 1991 against former WBA world heavyweight champion Mike Weaver in the USA at Caesars Tahoe in Nevada. While it was clear that Weaver was not the force of old, it would have been foolhardy to take him lightly. Since he was a puncher, such a fighter always represents a threat. There is a saying in boxing that the last thing a fighter loses is his punch and that has been proven correct on many an occasion. Weaver had a record which consisted of thirty-five wins, fifteen defeats, and one draw. Weaver's ring history was interesting in that he had challenged Larry Holmes for the WBC heavyweight crown at Madison Square Garden in New York on 22 June 1979, meeting with failure when he was stopped in round twelve. Weaver continued to set his sights high and fought his way back towards another shot at the title. His second challenge duly paid off when he won the WBA version of the crown on 31 March 1980, knocking out defending champion John Tate in round fifteen at the Stokley Athletics Center in Tennessee. Then, on 25 October 1980, he surrendered home-ground advantage and ventured to Bophuthatswana to make the first defence of his title at the Superbowl in Sun City, whereupon he knocked out South African Gerrie Coetzee in round thirteen to retain the crown. Weaver then made the second defence of his crown against the fancied James Tillis at the Horizon Arena in Rosemont, Illinois, winning on points after fifteen rounds on 3 October 1981. Then, at the Caesars Palace Sports Pavilion in Las Vegas on 10 December 1982, he came unstuck in his third outing as champion when he lost his title when stopped in round one by Michael Dokes. A return for the title took place on 20 May 1983 at the Dunes Hotel and Casino in Las Vegas, and while Weaver faired a great deal better this time around, pushing the champion all the way, he failed to regain the crown when the contest was declared a draw after fifteen rounds. Another world championship chance presented itself to Weaver on 15 June 1985 when he challenged the WBC heavyweight king Pinklon Thomas at the Riviera Hotel and Casino in Las Vegas. The challenge of Weaver came to a close in round eight when he was stopped by Thomas.

On the night that Lewis faced Weaver, it had to be admitted that he was not confronting the same man who had once defeated Coetzee, Tate, and Tillis, but the reflection of a once-dangerous fighter who still knew the moves, but was unable to execute them. Lewis was in full control from the start of the contest, outboxing his opponent and showing a good left jab that constantly found its target. In round five, cacophonous sounds came from some of the spectators who wanted to see more action from the two boxers. Punters who pay good money to see a fight are, of course, at liberty to show displeasure if they so desire—in this case, however, it appeared unwarranted, for both men were giving their best in a contest that may not have been full of blood and thunder, but was still interesting. Lewis eventually broke his opponent down, highlighting his potential and sheer class by knocking out his man in six rounds in a contest that was slated for ten.

At this time, it would not have surprised many if Weaver had thus decided to hang up his gloves and look for an easier profession. Nonetheless he fought on, having a further eight bouts, winning six and losing two. Weaver finally called it quits on 17 November 2000 when, in a return contest with former WBC and IBF heavyweight king Larry Holmes, he was stopped in the sixth round.

Glenn McCrory

It was time to put the gloves on once again to do battle and, on 30 September 1991, Lewis put his British and European titles on the line at the Royal Albert Hall. In the opposite corner was Glenn McCrory, the former IBF world, British, and Commonwealth cruiserweight champion from County Durham. Lewis was the favourite to continue his winning run and retain his titles, although McCrory was an experienced fighter with 28 victories and 6 defeats. A number of pundits felt that the challenger would not go down without making it a competitive fight and could well extend Lewis taking him into the later rounds.

McCrory had made a little boxing history by becoming the first British fighter to have won the world cruiserweight crown on 3 June 1989. McCrory was given the chance at the championship when the undisputed title holder at the weight, Evander Holyfield, relinquished the WBC, WBA, and IBF titles to move up to the heavyweight division. This then left the three versions of the championship up for grabs; McCrory outpointed Kenyan-born but Swiss resident Patrick Lumumba over twelve rounds for the vacant IBF version of the title. This was a great night for McCrory and British boxing. At the time, it really looked as if McCrory was going to have a lengthy reign since he appeared more than capable of being able to handle any future challengers in his division. It was also possible that McCrory could be involved in lucrative unification bouts against his then rival holders: Carlos de Leon of Puerto Rico (WBC), and Taoufik Belbouli (WBA) of France, who had captured other vacant championships at the poundage and looked beatable.

Glenn's first defence of the title on 21 October 1989 was a successful one, knocking out Siza Makhathini of South Africa in round eleven. The future for McCrory looked bright. However, in boxing, one should never think too far ahead, since one punch can change the landscape of dreams dramatically.

American Jeff Lampkin was the opponent who spoiled the party for McCrory and any grand designs that may have been planned for him. Lampkin provided a shock when he knocked out the Briton in the third round of his second title defence on 22 March 1990. Since that setback, McCrory had fought on just one occasion, in a contest that took place on 16 February 1991 and saw him score a two-round knockout victory over Terry Armstrong. McCrory looked impressive in victory, but Armstrong was leagues below Lewis. Glenn climbed into the ring to challenge Lewis, determined to unseat him from his titles and thus prove that he had a great deal to offer at heavyweight.

When the fight commenced, Lewis started quickly, looking sharp and very much in charge—every inch a world-class performer; a consummate professional who delivered his punches with dexterity coupled with power. Lewis remained champion when he retained his titles with a knockout in round two. McCrory tasted the full might of Lewis's punching ability in the opening session and finished the round with a bloody nose. McCrory bravely attempted to land blows of his own, but was not able to trouble Lewis at any time during the short period the contest lasted. McCrory was sent down to the canvas for a count in the second round prior to the right hand that Lewis landed to finish the job moments later. The right hand of Lewis was now looking a very fearful and dangerous weapon for any opponent who shared the ring with him—Lewis had used a similar right to put pay to Mike Weaver in his previous contest.

The boxing world was now taking a long and serious look at Lewis, who was becoming a genuine world contender. In some quarters there were a few reservations about how he would react when facing one of the top guns in the division. This is, of course, always a constant area of concern with up-and-coming fighters. While it is always good to vie on the side of caution in such matters, it really did look as if the British fighter was the genuine article who would be able to live up to the extremely high expectations that many had of him.

Tyrell Biggs

Lewis travelled to the USA for his next bout and appeared on the undercard of the Evander Holyfield's defence of the world heavyweight title against Bert Cooper. Lewis was set to trade leather with Tyrell Biggs in a contest scheduled for ten rounds at The Omni in Atlanta, Georgia, on 23 November 1991. It could be said that Lewis had a score to settle in this bout, since Biggs had eliminated him from the championships at the 1984 Olympics Games, which had taken place in Los Angeles. The American had outpointed Lewis in their bout and had gone on to win the gold medal at super-heavyweight by outpointing Italian Francesco Damiani in the final.

In the punch-for-pay ranks, Biggs had challenged Mike Tyson for the world heavyweight championship on 16 October 1987 in his sixteenth bout and was stopped in round seven. Tyson was too strong for Biggs, who found his amateur qualifications meant little against the defending champion, who punched him to a painful defeat. It could be said that after that loss Biggs was not the same fighter, suffering three defeats in his next seven outings. It is interesting to note that one of the respected setbacks was to the man Lewis took the British title from in 1991, Gary Mason, who knocked out the American in seven rounds in England on 4 October 1989. Prior to meeting the British fighter, Biggs had suffered a further loss on 2 March 1991 when stopped in round eight by future world heavyweight title holder Riddick Bowe.

A win for Lewis was the expected result, but how he looked achieving that victory was all-important as he had to put on a show in front of the American public. Lewis did not disappoint; he did a far better job than both Mason and Bowe when he gained revenge for his amateur defeat by stopping his rival in three punch-perfect rounds. Lewis put on a ruthless display and had put his man on the canvas three times with the referee halting the bout on the third knockdown. Once again, Lewis looked good and bossed the fight from the start; Biggs was not able to make any impression against the British fighter. The American had now lost two consecutive bouts to finalists from the 1988 Olympic Games, since Lewis had won gold and Bowe silver in the super-heavyweight division at the said event.

Levi Billups

Lewis engaged in another bout in the USA, meeting Levi Billups on 1 February 1992 at Caesars Palace in Las Vegas. The American did not represent a threat to Lewis in any shape or form, but he could not be taken for granted, as he had a record of sixteen wins and five defeats. No fighter should ever be underestimated, a fact that has been proven true many times to the cost of the favourite on the night. One of Billups's defeats came at the hands of former WBO light-heavyweight and future WBO, WBA, and IBF heavyweight world king Michael Moorer, who stopped him in three rounds on 25 June 1991. In his last bout before meeting Lewis, Billups had racked up a ten-round points victory over former WBA world heavyweight champion James Smith on 4 November 1991, which suggested that he had some ambition. Should Billups pull off an upset victory, it would most certainly propel him upwards in the world rankings and towards a slice of the big money on offer. Lewis was now the man to beat for a boxer wanting to make a name for themselves; the American had very little to lose and a great deal to gain. While Lewis was not able to stop his man inside the distance, he boxed in a controlled manner to continue his successful winning run by gaining a ten-round point's decision over Billups. This was the first time that the Briton had travelled this far in a contest. The victory helped Lewis to maintain his now high world ranking—taking him that one more step nearer to a world title fight.

Derek Williams

Lewis next climbed into the ring on 30 April 1992 at the Royal Albert Hall to defend his British and European titles in a twelve-round contest against Derek 'Sweet D' Williams, who would also be putting his Commonwealth crown on the line in the triple-championship meeting. Williams was also a former European champion having lost that title on 3 February 1990 to Jean-Maurice Chanet. Williams was a good fighter who had to be respected, but comparisons in their career at that stage revealed that he was not likely to be the first to defeat Lewis in the professional ranks. The Commonwealth champion had a record of nineteen wins and four defeats. For his contest with Lewis, Williams incorporated the services of the great American trainer Angelo Dundee, who was with him in the corner on the night. Dundee, while strongly associated with three-time world heavyweight king Muhammad Ali, had trained many other fine fighters during his remarkable career.

A victory for Lewis would see him win the treasured Lonsdale belt outright, a prize many UK British champions aim for. Lewis was determined to secure the win, but in the first and second rounds Williams boxed well and went to work quickly, using his left jab to good advantage and moving smoothly around the ring to keep out of harm's way. It was vital that Lewis did not let the man before him control the fight—he had to stamp his authority on the fight and thus take the initiative away from his opponent. Williams was no mug and was aware that, should he do the unexpected and win, his career would be on a new high. He would be flying, the toast of the town, in demand for big money fights.

Things did not remain so sweet for 'Sweet D' for in the third round. Lewis upped his game and showed his pedigree in no uncertain terms, scoring accurately with damaging punches to stop Williams in the stanza. Williams gave it his best shot, but, even with Dundee in his corner, he was not able to inflict the first defeat in the record of Lewis. Lewis once again showed in this contest that he was a class operator, pushing his unblemished record to a now impressive twenty, and, in doing so, becoming the outright owner of the Lonsdale belt—another prize for his trophy cabinet.

Above left: Frank Bruno (left) with manager Terry Lawless (centre) and stablemate Tony Adams (right) (*Derek Rowe*).

Above right: Frank Bruno always trained diligently for his fights, as George Butzbach found to his cost (*Derek Rowe*).

3 Frank Bruno (pictured) proved too strong for Eddie Neilson on 5 April 1983 (*Derek Rowe*).

Above left: Frank Bruno pictured with his European title belt after defeating Sweden's Anders Eklund (*Derek Rowe*).

Above right: Tim Witherspoon (pictured) spoiled the world title dreams of British fight fans when he defeated Frank Bruno (*Les Clark*).

Left: Frank Bruno, back on the world title trail after defeating James 'Quick' Tillis (*Les Clark*).

Right: Joe Bugner (pictured) was a man who had fought the best and looked a worthy opponent for Frank Bruno (*Derek Rowe*).

Below: Harry Carpenter (right) appears to be showing Frank Bruno which punch to throw (*Les Clark*).

Left: Frank Bruno (*pictured*) easily brushed opponent John Emmen aside in his first bout since being defeated by Mike Tyson (*Les Clark*).

Below: Jose Ribalta (right) on the ropes and no match for Frank Bruno (*Les Clark*).

Above: Pierre Coetzer (right) gave Frank Bruno a competitive night's work (*Les Clark*).

Below left: Frank Bruno (right) with Lennox Lewis (left) holding the WBC world title belt prize to their fight at Cardiff Arms Park (*Les Clark*).

Below right; Frank Bruno's phenomenal punching power could not be overlooked going into the all-British title fight. Lewis's grip on the belt was surely to be tested (*Les Clark*).

Above: Lennox Lewis (left), Frank Maloney (centre) and Frank Bruno (right) at the press conference prior to the 'Battle of Britain'—red, white, and blue was very much the colour scheme of choice (*Les Clark*).

Below: Frank Bruno talking to boxing historian Bert Randolph Sugar (*Les Clark*).

Right: Frank Bruno looking suave, his ambition finally achieved: he had won the WBC world heavyweight title (*Derek Rowe*).

Below: Frank Bruno signing autographs. He was always popular with fight fans (*Les Clark*).

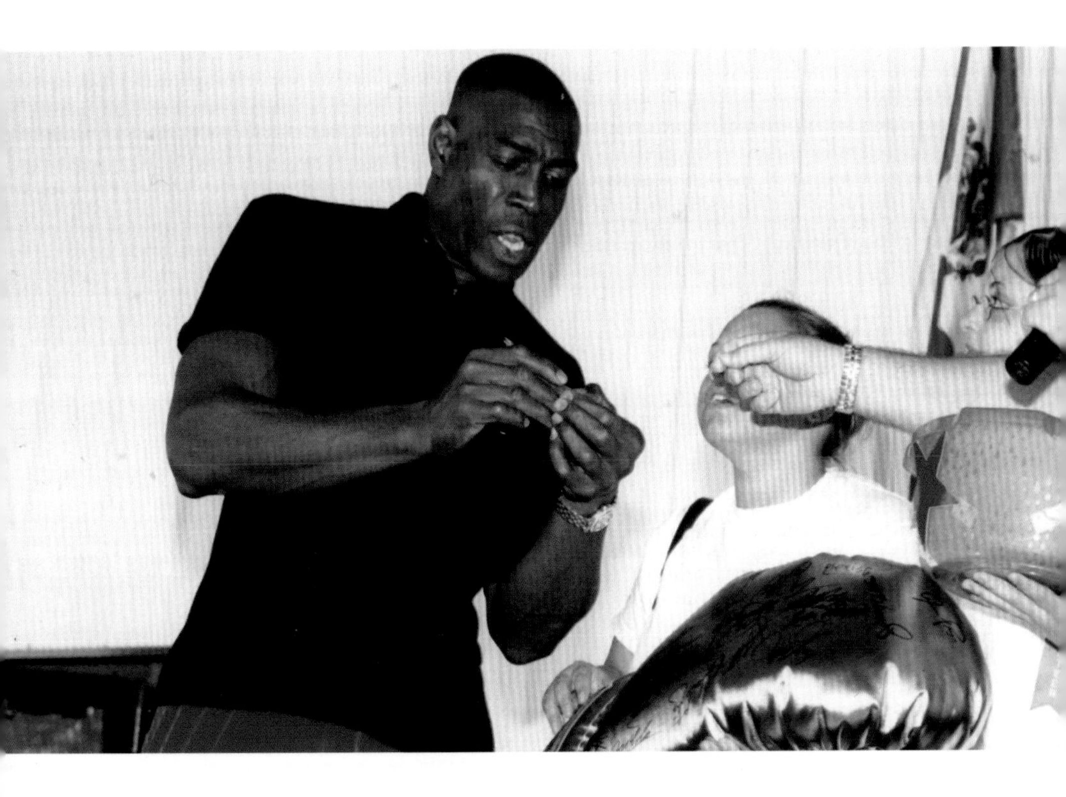

Above left: Frank Bruno, attending a dinner function, is applauded by fellow guests (*Philip Sharkey*).

Above right: Lennox Lewis carried quite the amateur pedigree into his professional career (*Les Clark*).

Below: Lennox Lewis (left), considered a real prospect by fight experts, being interviewed by Ian Darke (*Les Clark*).

Above left: Lennox Lewis continued his impressive winning run (*Les Clark*).

Above right: Lewis was always in top condition before a fight (*Les Clark*).

Below: Glen McCrory (left, with Muhammad Ali), was unable to handle the power of Lennox Lewis (*Derek Rowe*).

Above left: Donovan 'Razor' Ruddock looked to be a real threat to Lewis prior to their meeting (*Les Clark*).

Above right: Lennox Lewis sent out a message to the boxing world that he was the real deal when he easily defeated Ruddock (right) in two rounds (*Les Clark*).

Left: Lennox Lewis pictured with the world trophy. He was elevated to the status of WBC Heavyweight champion without throwing a punch (*Derek Rowe*).

Lennox Lewis became the first European fighter to win a world heavyweight title bout in America since Sweden's Ingemar Johansson—pictured in later years (*Les Clark*).

Lennox Lewis shows off his WBC world title belt prior to his much anticipated defence against Frank Bruno. Despite Bruno's power and valiant effort, Lewis's grip ultimately remained firmly on the WBC belt (*Les Clark*).

Above: Lennox Lewis (left) shakes hands with a serious-looking Frank Bruno (right) prior to their meeting in the ring (*Les Clark*).

Below: Lennox Lewis (left), looking relaxed at a press conference, like he belonged at the top of the heavyweight division. Frank Maloney (centre) and Frank Bruno look deep in concentration (*Les Clark*).

Above left: Oliver McCall shocked British boxing fans by unexpectedly defeating Lennox Lewis (*Les Clark*).

Above right: Henry Akinwande, pictured holding the Commonwealth Championship trophy, put himself in the running for a crack at Lennox Lewis by winning the WBO version of the world title (*Les Clark*).

Below: Herbie Hide adds to the British dominance of heavyweight boxing by regaining the WBO world heavyweight title, stopping former American IBF champion Tony Tucker (left) in two rounds for the vacant crown (*Les Clark*).

Above left: Shannon Briggs (pictured in later years) proved to be a dangerous opponent for Lennox Lewis (*Philip Sharkey*).

Above right: Challenger Željko Mavrović managed to last the distance with Lennox Lewis (*Les Clark*).

Above left: In defeating Evander Holyfield in their unification contest, Lennox Lewis became the undoubted number one fighter in the heavyweight division (*Les Clark*).

Above right: Despite his vast experience, Frans Botha was not able to compete with Lennox Lewis at any level (*Les Clark*).

Wladimir Klitschko looked to be a potential challenger for Lennox Lewis in the future (*Philip Sharkey*).

Above left: At last, the long-expected contest had arrived. Mike Tyson was to step into the ring with Lennox Lewis (*Les Clark*).

Above right: By capturing the WBA World Heavyweight title, Roy Jones Jnr looked a possible candidate to share the ring with Lennox Lewis (*Philip Sharkey*).

Above: Vitali Klitschko (left) knocked out Herbie Hide in two rounds to take the WBO World Heavyweight title (*Les Clark*).

Left: Muhammad Ali (left) stopping Henry Cooper in six rounds to retain his WBC heavyweight crown (*Derek Rowe*).

Mike Dixon

On 11 August 1992, a marking-time assignment to gain more experience of fighting in America took place at the Harrah's Marina Hotel Casino in Atlantic City. Opponent Mike Dixon, with a record of ten wins and five defeats, was the man coming out of the opposite corner in a contest set for ten rounds. In his previous bout on 9 July 1992, Dixon had lost a ten-round points decision to future WBA heavyweight king Bruce Seldon, and on 9 May 1992 he had lost to future WBO heavyweight champion Corrie Sanders by way of an eight-round points verdict.

Dixon took his chances against the undefeated British, European, and Commonwealth title holder, but was found wanting. Lewis held all the aces in this bout and was able to penetrate Dixon's defence with ease, scoring with both hands. The clash between the two was all over in round four, when the referee stepped in to stop the contest with the British fighter proving to be in a different league. Dixon was under pressure and taking heavy punishment in said stanza from Lewis, which resulted in him taking a count of eight. The fight continued for just a few moments more, when another sustained attack from Lewis clearly hurt Dixon and saw the referee stepping in to end the proceedings. This was the first time that Dixon had suffered a stoppage defeat in the paid ranks: the American had no answer to the classy and hard-hitting skills of the opponent he was facing. The cynical might say that the fight proved very little, which could not be disputed, but, on the plus side ,Lewis was keeping busy and that was a good thing.

At ringside, acting as a TV boxing analysis for the fight along with former WBA world lightweight champion Sean O'Grady and Al Albert, was Donovan 'Razor' Ruddock, who was more than just an interested observer. He was scheduled to be Lewis's next opponent.

Donovan 'Razor' Ruddock

The next fight for Lewis could be described as the most important and dangerous so far in his professional career. It was a defence of his Commonwealth title and a WBC title final eliminator—the winner would challenge the reigning holder, Evander Holyfield, for the title. Everything was riding on this contest; it was without doubt a boom or bust occasion. The opponent Lewis had to face was Canadian Donovan 'Razor' Ruddock, a fighter who had once defeated him in the amateur ranks.

Ruddock had proven his worth in the professional ranks by having fought

Mike Tyson in two hard-hitting battles. He had been stopped in round seven of their first encounter on 18 March 1991, then gone the full twelve-round distance with the fearsome former world champion in their second meeting on 28 June 1991. Ruddock's slate comprised an impressive twenty-seven victories, three defeats, and one draw. Ruddock had also impressively taken the scalps of four former WBA world heavyweight title holders: Mike Weaver, who he had outpointed over ten rounds on 23 August 1986; James Smith had failed to hear the final bell on 2 July 1989 when counted out in round seven; Michael Dokes was stopped in round four on 4 April 1990; and Greg Page, who retired in round eight on 15 February 1992. Ruddock was a man used to going in with fighters of a high calibre, and looked proficient enough to handle anything that Lewis would throw in his direction. The Canadian had also fought in the UK before, at the Alexandra Pavilion, Muswell Hill in London on 28 May 1986. On that occasion, Ruddock found the hospitality most welcoming when he came away with a seventh-round knockout victory. The opponent who had succumbed to the heavy fists of the Canadian visitor was Briton John Westgarth—a fine fighter, but not one in the class of Lewis it has to be said.

The outcome of the contest was far from certain. It was a wide open, even fight, and many felt that Ruddock could be the man to halt the march of Lewis towards the world title. If the British fighter had any deficiencies, Ruddock would be the man to exploit them. It had to be wondered at the time if some of the newspaper scribes were already secretly writing the obituary to Lewis's world title ambitions for their sports pages ahead of the big fight. It was not so much that they had no confidence in the home fighter's abilities, it was simply that Ruddock was a tough ask and a big hurdle to get over. Then there was the long, depressing list of the British heavyweights of the past who had crashed and burned when up against a world-class fighter. This fact played on the mind of many fight fans prior to the fight. Was it too much to expect Lewis to be any different and succeed where the others had failed? This was the acid test for Lewis, and the tension was running high at the Earls Court Exhibition Hall in Kensington. Those who had wanted Lewis to step up against a genuinely world-class fighter now had their wish, but was this that one step too far? Lewis had succeeded against good men like Gary Mason, Glenn McCrory, Tyrell Biggs, Jean-Maurice Chanet, Mike Weaver, etc., but Ruddock was a different proposition altogether and a very dangerous fighter.

During the introductions, Lewis looked calm. He could not have been cooler had he just stepped out of a freezer, which was incredible considering the importance of the fight he was about to take part in. The tension was electric; it was make-or-break time for the home fighter. Was Lewis the goods or was he only masquerading as a potential world heavyweight champion?

On the evening of 31 October 1992, Lewis produced a stunning victory far beyond anyone's wildest dreams when he stopped Ruddock in two sensational rounds. Lewis looked in a different class. In fact, he looked to be genuinely world class and way above Ruddock. The British fighter was in control from the start of the contest, confirming his punching power when unfurling a right hand that landed flush on Ruddock's chin, sending him crashing to the canvas, just moments before the bell sounded to end the session. Ruddock was felled twice more in the following round before the contest was halted.

It would have been considered an impressive achievement had Lewis won a close twelve-round points decision, but this was something special. Lewis had destroyed Ruddock, doing a better job than Mike Tyson had on the very same opponent. Ruddock may have been nicknamed 'Razor', but Lewis blunted his edge and was, without question, the sharper fighter on the night. He had sounded a stern warning to other fighters in the division that he was not a false alarm, but a man to be feared. If an army rank were to be attributed to the winner of this contest, one would have had to say that Lewis was a ring general, such was the authority of his display.

Britain now had a real heavyweight hopeful—a fighter who looked as if he really could deliver the goods and go all the way to the world heavyweight crown; Lewis had revealed against Ruddock all the prerequisite skills. This was a golden moment for British boxing, the likes of which the UK had not seen for some time.

The eyes of the boxing world were now firmly fixed on Lewis. He had emerged as one of the most exciting prospects in the division, providing a most vital blood transfusion to bolster the poundage, which at the time seemed to be anaemic. There is nothing like a good heavyweight on the scene to stimulate interest in the sport.

Lennox Lewis—World Champion

It now looked just a matter of time before Lewis faced champion Riddick Bowe in the ring. Bowe had impressed in taking the world crown from Evander Holyfield on 14 November 1992, by way of a twelve-round points decision for the championship. The hopes of all respective fight fans were running high that Lewis would repeat his amateur victory when the pair clashed. There was, however, a chain of thought from some quarters that a Lewis victory would not necessarily be a foregone conclusion. There was a world of difference between the unpaid code and the professionals; a second meeting between the two might very well have an entirely different outcome.

Such a sentiment may not have been welcomed by British fight fans, but it made sense, for there were a number of past cases in boxing supporting this theory that amateur victors could not repeat their wins when meeting the same opponent in a professional ring.

Any such rhetoric about the outcome of a proposed Lewis and Bowe bout proved to be a pointless exercise when the unexpected happened. At a press conference in London, Bowe relinquished the WBC portion of the crown by dropping that organisation's championship belt in a rubbish bin, but still retained both the WBA and IBF versions of the title. By this action, Bowe delayed any possible meeting with the WBC number-one contender. In response, the WBC swiftly proclaimed Lewis as their new champion based on his victory over Donovan 'Razor' Ruddock.

The bestowing of a title was not a unique act by that organisation. They had taken the same action when Leon Spinks agreed to defend his world heavyweight crown in a return bout against Muhammad Ali rather than against their number-one contender Ken Norton, who had won a WBC eliminator on 5 November 1977 by outpointing Jimmy Young over fifteen rounds. Spinks had been stripped of the WBC crown, leaving him with the WBA version—the WBC proclaimed Norton as their new champion based on his victory over Young.

This turn of events doubtless took away some of the expected accolades, glory, and gloss from Lewis's coronation as the new king, since he had been denied the opportunity of winning the championship inside the ring. The ring is where fighters much prefer to win the title, the battleground where the words '… and the new heavyweight champion of the world…' are heard. Having the title gift-wrapped and given to him in a boardroom somewhat demeaned his claim to the championship.

Despite this, Lewis was a world heavyweight champion; Britain's first since Bob Fitzsimmons. Lewis became the ninth non-American to hold a version of the title, following in the path of Bob Fitzsimmons in 1897–1899 (England); Tommy Burns in 1906–1908 (Canada); Max Schmeling in 1930–1932 (Germany); Primo Carnera in 1933–1934 (Italy); Ingemar Johansson in 1959–1960 (Sweden); Gerrie Coetze in 1983–1984 (South Africa); Trevor Berbick, who won and lost title in 1986 (Canada); and Francesco Damiani in 1989–1991 (Italy).

Lewis now had to prove beyond any doubt that he was a worthy champion by taking on the best available contenders—and hopefully obtain a unification bout with Riddick Bowe at a future date. That was a contest he dearly desired and one that would determine who the best fighter in the division was.

At that moment in time, Lewis also became the eighth Olympic gold medallist to have held a version of the world heavyweight crown. The previous holders were Floyd Patterson (middleweight, 1952); Cassius Clay, later Muhammad Ali (light-heavyweight, 1960); Joe Frazier (heavyweight, 1964); George Foreman (heavyweight, 1968); Leon Spinks (light-heavyweight, 1976); Michael Spinks (middleweight, 1976); and Ray Mercer (heavyweight, 1988).

Tony Tucker

They say, 'what happens in Vegas stays in Vegas'—the famed city where fortunes are won and lost overnight, be it on the turn of the card, the roll of the dice, or the spin of the roulette wheel. Would Lewis become a casualty of Las Vegas? Was it a gamble to make the first defence of his world title in 'Sin City'?

The stakes were high. Ken Norton, who had been elevated to champion like Lewis, lost his WBC heavyweight crown in his first defence, when outpointed over fifteen rounds by Larry Holmes on 9 June 1978. Norton had met defeat in Las Vegas at Caesars Palace. Was history going to repeat itself?

The Briton put his crown on the line against former IBF world heavyweight champion Tony Tucker on 8 May 1993 at the Thomas & Mack Center in Las Vegas. This was no easy first defence for Lewis—Tucker was not a soft option and more than just a worthy contender. Tucker was a most capable fighter with ambition, and had not come to the ring just for a payday or to help enhance the reputation of Lewis. The American's record read forty-eight wins, one no contest, and one defeat—statistics that warned this man was for real, and in no rush to register a second defeat on his impressive CV.

Tucker had won the vacant IBF world heavyweight crown on 30 May 1987, by stopping James Douglas in round ten. The lone defeat came when he lost his IBF crown by a twelve-round points decision in a unification title bout with the then reigning WBC and WBA king Mike Tyson. This battle of champions took place on 1 August 1987. Tuckers' tenure as champion may not have lasted too long, but the defeat was no disgrace—it confirmed his durability, since those were the days when few fighters lasted the distance against the powerful punching Tyson, who put his opponents away in double-quick time. Tucker had successfully defended the NABF heavyweight crown on 26 June 1992 by outpointing future WBC world champion Oliver McCall over twelve rounds.

Some pundits seriously wondered if the reign of Lennox was going to be short-lived against a challenger fighting on his own turf, with home support giving him that extra lift with their cheers. Thus, the American fans hoped that Tucker would defeat Lewis and bring the WBC portion of the world title back to the States where they felt it rightfully belonged—this would then see an all-American unification fight with Bowe somewhere down the line.

Many British heavyweights had failed dismally in the USA when faced with a top-notch operator. The last British fighter to contest the heavyweight championship of the world in America was Frank Bruno, who challenged Mike Tyson at the Las Vegas Hilton on 25 February 1989. Bruno was not given much chance of victory prior to the fight and was predicted to be defeated by the heavily favoured champion inside the distance—he was stopped in round five. Was Lewis heading for the same canyon of pain and despair? Was he fated to add his name to the list of defeated limey heavyweights in the USA? Some thought he just might. Despite his obvious skill set, there was a still a nagging thought that it might all go wrong for the Lewis.

However, Lewis proved that notion wrong—he was one heavyweight from the UK who had not come to fail. While Tucker was no pushover, the British fighter did the business and performed well, flooring Tucker twice during the contest in round three and nine—Tucker had reportedly never been put down for a count before in a contest—and in doing so answered any lingering doubts about his right to the championship. In outpointing his challenger over twelve rounds, Lewis cemented his status as a *bona fide* title holder.

The victory over Tucker made Lewis the first British-born heavyweight to win in a world title contest on American soil since Bob Fitzsimmons, who won the crown on 17 March 1897 by knocking out defending champion James J. Corbett in round fourteen at the Race Track Arena in Carson City. The last European to win a world heavyweight title in the USA prior to Lewis was Sweden's Ingemar Johansson, who had stopped defending champion Floyd Patterson in three rounds to win the title on 26 June 1959 at the Yankee Stadium in New York. It really was exceptionally rare to see an American defeated on home ground for the world heavyweight crown. Lewis looked set to bring new respect to the image of British heavyweights in the states.

Lewis Puts Pressure on Bowe

The reign of Lewis put pressure on WBA and IBF king Riddick Bowe. Bowe was, in the eyes of many, the real world champion—the number one heavyweight in the division who had won his titles in the ring and was therefore recognised as the legitimate king. While it was difficult to argue with this view, it was apparent that Lewis was (to some extent) upstaging Bowe and stealing his thunder, hence validating his own claim to being the best heavyweight on the planet.

Bowe appeared to be making title defences against easier opposition than Lewis. Bowe had put his titles on the line on 6 February 1993 against former WBA king Mike Dokes. Dokes had had his ups and downs in his career since being champion, and was a reasonable choice for Bowe's first-time defence—Dokes had won his last nine bouts in a row, which made him a credible challenger. However, he was in no way a serious threat to Bowe's crown—a fact that was painfully proved true when Bowe, without great effort, brushed aside his man in the opening round. It was then expected that Bowe, in his second outing as champion, would meet a more testing opponent—a challenger who represented more of a threat. Nonetheless, on 22 May 1993, a fighter who did not in any shape or form merit a crack at the crown, Jesse Ferguson, was brought in to face Bowe. Bowe was not troubled by his opponent, stopping him in round two. Ferguson may have lasted longer than Dokes, but that did not make him a viable or deserving challenger. Only the WBA gave recognition to this defence; the IBF failed to sanction the bout. Ferguson came into the ring against Bowe having won just three of his last eight bouts, which were hardly the kind of credentials to challenge for a world heavyweight championship. It was no surprise to anyone that the fight ended so quickly and that Riddick Bowe was still the title holder when the dust had settled. While Bowe was an undoubtedly a good fighter, these kind of matches did little to enhance his reputation.

Frank Bruno

Lewis next put his championship on the line in the open air at Cardiff Arms Park on 1 October 1993, in an all-British showdown against challenger Frank Bruno. This was a historical boxing occasion for it was the first time that two British-born boxers had fought for a version of the championship and the first heavyweight title bout to take place in Wales. While Lewis was the favourite to retain the crown, Bruno—the former European champion with a record of thirty-six wins and three defeats—was a dangerous puncher, with thirty-five of his victories coming inside the distance by a stoppage or a knockout. Bruno was a man who could not be underestimated; this was to be his third challenge for a world heavyweight crown, having failed with a valiant attempt in the eleventh round after challenging Tim Witherspoon for the WBA crown on 19 July 1986. Bruno had then come up short once again on 25 February 1989, when stopped by Mike Tyson in five rounds for the undisputed crown.

The evening may have been chilly, an earlier rainfall ensuring that the UK had no water shortage and that the trusty umbrella was fully employed, but despite the far-from-desirable weather conditions, the fans' enthusiasm was not dampened in any way. This was a meeting the fans wanted to see—they were not disappointed by what was about to take place inside the ring.

In the early stages of this adrenaline-filled contest, Bruno boxed extremely well, giving his opponent various problems with a variation of crisp, accurate shots that landed on target. Bruno was working well, building up a points lead that must have given the champion's corner some concern. The challenger continued to impress as the rounds passed, using his solid left jab to good effect, giving the suggestion that perhaps the title might change hands. While Lewis was an excellent fighter, Bruno was a sentimental favourite with the fans and many watching the match were heartily cheering him on. To some extent, Bruno's boxing skills were underrated. When combined with his potent punching power, he was a fighter more than capable of ending the bout should he connect cleanly. Lewis had to ensure that there was no lapse in his defence and that his chin was not left hanging out to dry.

Bruno continued to look good in the early rounds of the contest and pressed the title holder hard. Soon, however, the champion's undoubted class started to shine through; he found his rhythm and stepped up a gear, bringing his own heavy punching into play to retain the championship with a stoppage in round seven (Bruno went on to win the WBC heavyweight crown in future fights). The fight lived up to all expectations, with both champion and challenger providing the fans with a good night's action. Lewis was still WBC champion of the world, and bigger bouts were on the horizon.

While Lewis was keenly eyeing a unification contest against WBA and IBF king Riddick Bowe, a shock occurred when, on 6 November 1993 at Caesars Palace, Evander Holyfield regained the titles with a twelve-round points decision. It could be said, without fear of contradiction, that no one saw it coming. It now looked as if Lewis would have to set his sights on Holyfield, which would still be a good bout if both parties could come to an agreement. Before any such plans could come to any possible fruition, the championship changed hands once again, when Michael Moorer relieved Holyfield of the titles by way of a twelve-round points decision at Caesars Palace on 22 April 1994.

Hide Captures WBO World Heavyweight Crown

Prior to the Moorer-Holyfield title clash, an interesting development took place on 19 March 1994. At the New Den in Millwall, London, another British fighter in the shape of Herbie Hide won the WBO version of the heavyweight crown, knocking out holder Michael Bentt in seven rounds. Strangely enough, Bentt had been born in London but was brought up in the USA, and thus was considered an American fighter. At that time, the WBO was something of a fledging organisation with their first heavyweight title bout having taken place on 6 May 1989. Italy's Francesco Damiani became their first champion at the weight by knocking out South African Johnny Du Plooy in three rounds—Hide thus became their sixth title holder. The previous champions were American's Ray Mercer, Michael Moorer, Tommy Morrison, and Bentt. Hide looked to be an interesting addition to the top tier of the heavyweight mix.

Phil Jackson

Lewis next entered the warzone on 6 May 1994 at the Broadwalk Convention Center in Atlantic City to trade leather with Phil Jackson, a capable fighter with a record of thirty wins and one defeat—that lone loss being to Canada's Donavan 'Razor' Ruddock, the man Lewis had destroyed in two thrilling rounds on 31 October 1992. Jackson had entered the fray with Ruddock on 26 June 1992 to contest the vacant IBC heavyweight crown, but failed in his bid when knocked out in round four. Despite that setback, Jackson hoped he could produce the goods to bring the WBC crown back to the USA, where many stateside fans still firmly felt it belonged.

Since the defeat to Ruddock, the American had won five bouts on the bounce and looked a more mature fighter. Credit had to be given to Lewis when defending the championship—he was not meeting soft touches, but opponents with solid winning records who were keen to rip the title away from him. The American gave his best, but the championship qualities of Lewis ensured that he returned to Britain with his crown intact. Lewis was never troubled by his opponent, putting his man on the deck in the opening stanza and flooring him twice in the fifth round whereupon he had a point deducted. The point was taken by the referee when one of the knockdowns in the stanza occurred after the bell sounded to end the round. The action was not a cheap shot, or indeed an act of malice on the part of Lewis, but one of exuberance in the heat of battle. The loss of a point was not a massive setback for the British fighter, since he was in full flow and well in command of the fight, landing with hurtful punches. Another victory for the champion looked assured as each minute passed. Lewis finally concluded the defence of his title by flooring Jackson once again in round eight, forcing the referee to stop the bout in his favour. The contest was scheduled for twelve rounds, but it never looked like going the distance. Lewis had bossed the contest from the off, and was at no time in danger of incurring his first professional defeat.

Oliver McCall (I)

Lewis's next challenge took place on home ground against American Oliver McCall; the two met at Wembley Arena on 24 September 1994. McCall, nicknamed 'Atomic Bull', was not what could be called a walkover defence, but it was generally felt that, while he should be given every respect, he was not considered too dangerous an opponent. Truth be told, McCall did not look that special—not a man who appeared likely to return to the USA as champion. If Lewis was to be beaten, it would be by a fighter who had built a reputation with impressive wins—a puncher with an undefeated record over quality opponents. That was the general opinion. It looked as if McCall was destined to follow the fate of Lewis's previous challengers: Tony Tucker, Frank Bruno, and Phil Jackson.

McCall came with a record of twenty-four wins and five defeats. One of the American's notable victories came on 23 April 1993 when he stopped in round eight Italy's former WBO world heavyweight champion, Francesco Damiani. This showed that the challenger to Lewis had some pop in his punches.

McCall's demeanour before the contest started suggested that he was clearly not in England for the fun of it, or to be another victim to fall at the hands of Lewis without making a fight of it. He wanted the championship badly, as indeed all contenders for the title do, but McCall appeared to have a burning anger inside him that made him more of a threat than previously thought. In his corner, McCall had the well-respected trainer Emanuel Steward, a man who had taken a number of fighters to world crowns in various weight divisions, and was more often than not in the victor's corner when a fight was over. Make no mistake: Steward knew the fight game back to front; a true master of his profession.

When the bout got underway, the challenger looked unfazed and it was obvious in the first round that the growing reputation of Lewis held no fears for him. McCall threw heavy-looking rights hands at the title holder's head during the opening session that were avoided with ease, but one did not need to be a boxing expert to know that the American's blows were getting closer and would do a great deal of damage if they found their target and landed cleanly. Despite this, most of the fans watching were relaxed, and believed that Lewis would soon put the challenger in his place, for he seemed an unsinkable class above. Lewis appeared to be the *Titanic* of the division, a man set to reign as heavyweight champion for some time.

Round two commenced with Lewis looking confident, biding his time, and looking to stamp his authority on the contest. However, a dramatic change to the career path of the Briton took place when McCall's right hand cut its way through the champion's defence, putting him down on the canvas for the first time in his professional career. On beating the count and getting to his feet, the referee judged that the British fighter had not recovered sufficiently from the punch, and stopped the bout in the American's favour. Lewis was far from happy about the decision, but he could do little to change it—he was to leave the ring as a former champion. If Lewis was at that time the division's *Titanic,* then McCall had been his iceberg, claiming Lewis's world title along with his undefeated record. It was difficult to believe that the reign of Lewis was at an end.

Once the dust had settled, plans to regain the title were put into action. However, it was clear that there would be no quick fix and no immediate return with McCall—Lewis was not going to be handed any favours. He had to do it the hard way and fight his way back into contention to earn his shot. Some critics felt that the world championship days of Lewis were over. While this was not pleasant to hear or read, it had to be admitted that such a depressing view did hold a degree of substance since few titles holders in the division returned after such a defeat.

However, the British fighter's views on the subject were positive. He was a fighter, in every sense of the word, and had every intention of wearing the crown again. He was determined that he would not sink without a trace. For him, the final bell had not yet rung.

George Foreman Regains Crown

It was all change at the top of the heavyweight division once again when, on 5 November 1994, former world champion George Foreman did the unthinkable and knocked out Michael Moorer in round ten at the MGM Grand, Las Vegas, to regain the WBA and IBF versions of the world title. This was a most unexpected result, especially so when considering that Foreman had lost the undisputed crown to Muhammad Ali via a knockout in round eight on 30 October 1974 at The Stade du 20 Mai in Kinshasa, Democratic Republic of Congo. Foreman was now a world champion again, after an incredible period of twenty years and six days. In so doing, Foreman made fistic history, by becoming the oldest man to win the heavyweight crown at the age of forty-five years, nine months and twenty-six days. Many had felt that the golden days of Foreman were a thing of the past, his name having been gently laid to rest with the many other bygone heroes of the square ring. Those who thought that (and there were many it has to be said) felt the former champion was in for a beating on the night. Who could blame them for such a view, considering Foreman's age? Moorer had youth—he was twenty-six years, eleven months and twenty-four days old—he had speed, and he was an awkward southpaw. He had everything in his favour. How could he not win? It was staggering to think that when Foreman made his professional debut on 23 June 1969, stopping Don Waldheim in three rounds, Moorer was only one year, seven months and eleven days old. Moorer looked a certain winner, a man set to finally banish Foreman from boxing forever with an overwhelming victory.

Those who felt Foreman had no chance were spectacularly wrong. Foreman sent out the message that nothing was impossible and that the game was not over just because he had passed forty, far from it. The man was a walking inspiration to both those in and outside the ring. Foreman had shown that he was by no means a spent force, a fighter not yet ready to throw his last punch, nor ready for carpet slippers, slow walks in the park, and a rocking chair. He still had a great deal left in the locker; his competitive urge had not vanished with the passing of time. Foreman had also shown that the old boxing adage, 'they never come back', is not always correct. Foreman had made his return to the ring on 9 March 1987, stopping opponent Steve Zouski in round four after retiring from the sport following a twelve-round points defeat to Jimmy Young on 17 March 1977. Fight pundits at the time felt that Foreman was making a big mistake in returning to the ring, one that would eventually see him defeated and sent back into retirement by a young pup on the way up.

Many men of Foreman's age must have been pleased when they heard that he had duly sent Moorer to sleep; it surely gave them a spring in their step for a couple of days. It also gave the doubters cause to re-think the Lewis situation. After all, if Foreman could do the unthinkable and regain the title at an advanced age after so many years, who would be brave enough to say that, in the unpredictable sport of boxing, Lewis would not march on and also take the championship once again?

Riddick Bowe Back in the Running

On 11 March 1995, former undisputed champion Riddick Bowe put his name back on the list of reigning title holders when he took the remaining version of the world crown from British hands, by defeating title holder Herbie Hide. Bowe did this by way of a six-round knockout to win the WBO heavyweight title at the MGM Grand in Las Vegas. Bowe looked good in victory, showing impressive punching power and looking more than ready to play with the other major contenders in the division. The win confirmed that the man was still very much a major force in the heavyweight poundage. The boxing fraternity was united in the hope that a Bowe and Lewis showdown would still take place in the ring at a later date, to settle once and for all who the better fighter was. It was a match crying out to be made, a major fight attraction wherever it would be staged. Lewis, however, had his own agenda: to regain the WBC world heavyweight crown.

Lionel Butler

The start on the long road back to redemption for Lewis began on 13 May 1995 at the Arco Arena, Sacramento, USA, in a WBC eliminator against Lionel Butler. The date of the fight was a significant one in heavyweight boxing history, as it had been on this day in 1914 that the great Joe Louis was born—a man who notched a record twenty-five defences of the world heavyweight crown.

It was obvious that no one was going to open the door easily for the former champion in his bid to regain the crown. In what can only be described as a clever move, Lewis incorporated the services of a new trainer in the shape of American Emanuel Steward, replacing Puerto Rican Pepe Correa. The man was a legend in his trade—an undoubted asset in the corner of any fighter. This was the same trainer who had helped to plot Lewis's downfall when in the opposing corner of Oliver McCall on the fateful night he unexpectedly lost his world crown.

Butler was beatable and not what one would call a serious threat to the former WBC king. The American was not a man who would cause Lewis to hide behind the sofa or suffer another loss on his record. It was more than apparent that Lewis had fought and beaten better opponents during his career; a glaring fact any student of boxing would have observed prior to the fight. However, coming back after an unexpected defeat, a fighter can often be mentally fragile and vulnerable if he has failed to shake off the effects of his last loss. Boxers are human after all, and not unemotional machines or robots that enter the ring to perform without thought or consequence. Over the years, a number of top-notch fighters in various weight divisions have failed to scale the lofty heights they had formerly held before their bubble burst. A boxer must be fit in both mind and body to do battle.

At any other time, critics would surely have claimed that the American was made to order for Lewis. An easy night's work, no more than a warm-up bout to keep him sharp—an opinion that one would have to go along with. The American had won 22 bouts, lost 10, drawn 1, with 1 no contest. Butler had mixed with top company before having previously exchanged punches with the likes of future world heavyweight king Riddick Bowe on 6 March 1989, losing when stopped in round two. Butler had also suffered a ten-round points defeat to future WBC world heavyweight title holder Oliver McCall on 16 July 1990. Butler then started to turn his career around when he knocked out former WBA world heavyweight champion Tony Tubbs in the first round on 18 August 1992. A meeting with James Smith, the former WBA world heavyweight title holder, proved to be a successful assignment when he stopped him in the third round on 18 January 1994.

The American fighter held no fear of Lewis. He perhaps felt the Briton was ready for the taking and this was his big chance to make a statement, especially when considering the circumstances of Lewis's last contest. There were no two ways about it: Lewis needed to win and look good in doing so. A dull victory would not help his cause, and defeat was clearly not an option. If he crashed and burned on this outing, it would be all over. Butler was clearly part of the key required to open the door towards regaining the world title. Lewis had been bombed out by McCall in two dramatic rounds to lose his WBC crown and his undefeated record, which then stood at twenty-five bouts. He had to put that dramatic episode behind him and lay that ghost to rest if he was to succeed. Any thoughts of self-doubt had to be eradicated from the mind—however, this is often easier said than done, and it is very difficult to perform when under fire in the heat of battle. When the bell rings to start the contest, all the wise words of a trainer can dissipate the instant the opponent comes menacing forward, throwing punches.

When the fight got underway, Lewis came briskly out of his corner, showing strength of both mind and character by boxing in a confident manner. Lewis was determined to get back on track and shake off the McCall defeat. Lewis boxed well, using his left jab to good effect and throwing the occasional right hand while at the same time remaining cautious of what was coming back from his opponent. Lewis did not want a repeat of the McCall fight and to walk into a punch that spelled goodnight. Lewis showed that he was not ready to add another defeat against his name, and duly fought his way back into the win column with a five-round stoppage over the American.

During the bout, Lewis was able to prise over the defence of Butler and land his telling blows without difficulty. While the fight was not exceptionally exciting, Lewis put in a workman-like performance to get the job done and thus get himself back among the contenders for his old title. The contest was scheduled for twelve rounds, but Lewis was determined that the bout would not last that long. Lewis had cleared the first hurdle and the turning of a key in the lock had been heard.

Justin Fortune

Australian Justin Fortune was the next opponent to go up against Lewis, on 2 July 1995 at the Point in Dublin, Ireland, in a contest slated for ten rounds. Fortune, with a record of eleven wins, two defeats, and one draw, did not look to be a threat, since he clearly did not have the necessary experience or the punching power to inconvenience the former WBC world champion, who had met fighters of a higher calibre. Fortune had won the Australian-New South Wales State heavyweight title by outpointing American-born holder Jack Johnson over ten rounds on 10 May 1991. On 8 May 1992, he added the vacant OPBF heavyweight crown to his name via the disqualification of his opponent, August Tanuvasa of New Zealand, in round two.

Fortune had fought in the USA on six occasions, gaining three wins, one draw, and two defeats. The fights had taken place against moderate opposition, with the exception of Buster Mathis Jnr, who was then considered a prospect. Mathis Jnr had stopped the Australian in round eight on 14 February 1993.

Fortune had also plied his wares in England with some success. On 26 June 1993, he knocked out opponent Vance Idiens in the first round, barely breaking a sweat. On 28 July 1993, he scored another inside-the-distance victory, this time over Chris Harbourne, who he knocked out in round three. These opponents were good ring operators, but nowhere need world class—certainly nowhere near the class of Lewis. However, it was evident that Fortune was no stranger to fighting away from home. The Australian could, to some extent, produce the goods at a lower level, but Lewis looked to be that one level too much. The bout against Lewis was considered to be Fortune's big chance; should the fighter from down under spring an upset, it would be a major news story and a shocking setback for the British fighter. Nonetheless, it has to be said that he really had less chance of victory than Custer had at the Battle of Little Bighorn in 1876. Indeed, the odds on Custer would have been more favourable.

Fortune had nothing to lose going into the bout; he was considered a defeated man long before he had even put the gloves on. There have been a number of times in boxing when the underdog has overcome the odds to score a shocking victory, but not on this night. All predictions were spot on and Lewis won in a canter by stopping his man in round four. On this occasion, Fortune found that the only fortune he had with him in the ring was his name. The Australian did his best and made a fight of it, but the gap in class between the two boxers was too wide for him to bridge. While this was deemed an easy assignment for Lewis, cynics might well ask what it proved. The answer was clear: very little, but it kept Lewis busy, and who in truth could begrudge the Briton the occasional easy outing? Especially when considering the top-notch fighters he had formerly shared the ring with, and the other top-league boxers he was due to meet in his quest to regain the heavyweight championship of the world.

Tommy Morrison

Keeping busy, Lewis once again travelled to the USA, to meet former WBO world heavyweight king Tommy Morrison on 7 October 1995 at the Convention Centre in Atlantic City. The American looked to be a tough fight—a much tougher one than the last Lewis had participated in, with Justin Fortune.

Morrison had an impressive record of forty-five wins, two defeats, and one draw. He had victories over quality—men of the ring like former world heavyweight champion George Foreman, who he had defeated on 7 June 1993 by way of a twelve-round points decision to win the vacant WBO crown. The win over Foreman was Morrison's second crack at the title; his first tilt came on 18 October 1991 when the then defending champion, Ray Mercer, stopped him in round five. After beating Foreman for the crown, Morrison looked like having a lengthy reign as champion. In his first defence of the title on 30 August 1993, he stopped challenger Tim Tomashek, who retired in round four. Then, unexpectedly, he lost the crown in his second defence when stopped in the first round on 29 October 1993 by Michael Bentt in a shock result. Morrison also had on his record a victory over former WBC heavyweight king Pinklon Thomas, who retired in the first round on 19 February 1991. The indications were that the American was by no means a spent force and he had plenty of fight left in him. Morrison, in his last contest (10 June 1995) before stepping in with Lewis, had stopped Donovan 'Razor' Ruddock in round six to take the vacant IBC heavyweight crown.

Lewis was aware that Morrison would be a good name to add to his record. By the same token, Morrison knew that a win over Lewis would energise his career and put him back among the main players in the division and in line for another crack at the world heavyweight crown. A defeat for Lewis would be a disaster, perhaps even a career-ending one. Lewis was walking a tightrope in each contest he undertook.

Morrison went to war from the start of the contest, throwing plenty of leather—Lewis met him head-on and fought fire with fire. In an exciting battle, which was turning into an all-out slugfest, Lewis was superb, showing all his class to crush Morrison in six hard-hitting rounds. Morrison was floored for a count in rounds two, five, and then twice in round six. The fight was a punishing one for Morrison, who finished the bout showing the signs of battle, with cuts over the right eye and under the left. The contest was scheduled for twelve rounds, but such was the ferocity right from the start it hardly looked like going the full distance. This was a performance that suggested the British fighter had every chance of one day wearing the world crown once more if given the opportunity. The contest was billed as being for the IBC heavyweight title, which Lewis later relinquished.

Ray Mercer

Lewis was really doing things the hard way. In his next contest, on 10 May 1996, he shared the ring with yet another former WBO world heavyweight champion. His opponent was an American in the fighting form of Ray Mercer, a man who, like Lewis, had competed at the 1988 Olympic Games in Seoul, winning a gold medal in the heavyweight division. This bout was going to be far from an easy night's work.

Mercer, nicknamed 'Merciless', was a tough man who would give anyone a battle and had not entered the ring just to occupy the opposite corner. He was there to win and blast Lewis into oblivion. The bout was not one in which a Lewis victory would be tipped with confidence; Mercer had a record of twenty-three wins, three defeats and one draw, after mixing with the likes of former WBA cruiserweight champion Ossie Ocasio of Puerto Rico, who he outpointed over eight rounds on 7 December 1989. The high point of his career came when he won the WBO world heavyweight championship, knocking out holder Francesco Damiani of Italy in round nine on 11 January 1991. A first successful defence of the title followed on 18 October 1991, when he turned back the challenge of Tommy Morrison by way of a five-round stoppage. Soon after, Mercer relinquished the WBO championship and later met former WBC and IBF king Larry Holmes on 7 February 1992, wherein he met with his first defeat after being outpointed over twelve rounds by his vastly experienced foe. Evander Holyfield was also a class name to note—Mercer met the former undisputed world champion on 20 May 1995 and lost a ten-round points decision.

The encounter between Lewis and Mercer took place at Madison Square Garden, New York, and proved to be a showdown to remember—a bruising battle with both fighters having to really pull out all the stops. Both combatants made a visit to the land of pain, often going toe-to-toe when exchanging punches. In the later stages the fight developed into a war of attrition, with both men having to dig down into their fighting soul and find that little bit extra in their efforts to win. Lewis and Mercer showed that their jaws were not made of glass by each taking a few solid blows without blinking or seeking refuge on the canvas. The fans in attendance were treated to an exciting scrap and really got value for their money, with both men putting it on the line.

At the end of ten close and exciting rounds, Lewis was given a points decision in what had to be one of his hardest battles in the paid ranks. The 'Big Apple' appearance for Lewis was successful, but Mercer without doubt took the British boxer close, and it looked at times as if he was going to be the second man to defeat him, and thus end his advance towards becoming a world champion for a second time. It was a rough and rugged night, but these are the kind of bouts that often define a fighter and make him a more complete performer in the ring.

Henry Akinwande WBO King

On 29 June 1996, Henry Akinwande brought the WBO version of the world heavyweight crown back to the UK, when he knocked out American Jeremy Williams in three rounds for the vacant title at the Fantasy Springs Casino in Indio, California. Akinwande was a good technical boxer, and, although not noted for his punching power, in this bout he showed that he could land the pay-off punch if the opportunity presented itself—a plus factor when going into any contest. In the bout with Williams, Akinwande boxed well, giving a performance that suggested he and Lewis might very well meet at a future date in an all-British showdown with championship belts on the line.

Oliver McCall (II)

The chance for Lewis to regain the WBC world heavyweight championship took place on 7 February 1997 at the Hilton Hotel in Las Vegas. The title had been vacated by Mike Tyson, and the opposition Lewis was to face was none other than Oliver McCall, the man who had defeated him to take the crown on 24 September 1994.

After beating Lewis, McCall had made a successful defence against former WBC and IBF champion Larry Holmes, winning a twelve-round points victory on 8 April 1995, only to lose the crown in his second defence against Frank Bruno on 2 September 1995 by a twelve-round points decision. Since the Bruno setback, McCall bounced back with two victories inside the distance: a first-round stoppage over future WBC world heavyweight champion Oleg Maskaev on 24 February 1996, and a five-round retirement victory over James Stanton on 23 March 1996. These took his record to twenty-eight wins and six defeats. The American looked primed and ready to do battle with his British opponent; the scene was set for a contest between two well-matched fighters with a burning desire to be crowned champion for a second time. To some degree, it must have been a matter of concern for McCall to know that Lewis now had the excellent trainer Emanuel Steward with him in the corner. The last time he and Lewis fought, Steward was in his corner—would this give his rival a slight edge?

In the early rounds of the bout, McCall looked as if he was going to give Lewis a strong and testing time, the psychological bonus of having a previous victory over the British fighter helping to kindle his fighting spirit. McCall showed no hesitation from the first bell and threw punches at Lewis, looking for the one that would explode on the Briton's chin. Rounds two and three suggested that Lewis was getting on top.

Something incredible happened in round four. McCall started to walk away, not throwing any kind of threatening punch at his opponent. He appeared to have lost the will to fight. Lewis landed with solid rights to the head of his opponent with little response. McCall backed off and continued to show little interest in engaging with Lewis in what was now becoming a ridiculously one-sided affair.

Just when there seems to be nothing unseen left in boxing, something surprising jumps up. This was one such occasion.

In round five, the referee had finally seen enough, and stepped in to stop the contest (it was later reported that McCall had a breakdown in the ring). Under the circumstances, it was not an ideal way to win, and this robbed Lewis to some extent of a glorious victory. In truth, this was not the fault of the British fighter. At the end of the day, Lewis won the prize and the jackpot that came with it: being crowned once again the WBC world heavyweight champion and the first European boxer to regain a title in this division.

Hide Regains WBO Championship

Britain's dominance in the division continued when Herbie Hide regained the vacant WBO world heavyweight crown by stopping former IBF world king Tony Tucker in round two (the title had been previously relinquished by Henry Akinwande). The Hide–Tucker contest took place at the Sports Village in Norwich, Norfolk, on 28 June 1997. It was a good win for Hide—one that once again saw him back as champion. However, it was clear that the Tucker who confronted Hide was only a shadow of the man who had once shared the ring with the likes of James Douglas, Mike Tyson, and Lennox Lewis. Following this victory, it had to be wondered if Hide and Lewis would eventually cross gloves in the future.

Henry Akinwande

The first defence Lewis made in his second reign took place on 12 July 1997 against fellow British fighter Henry Akinwande, a former European, Commonwealth, and WBO world heavyweight champion. Akinwande had an excellent record, winning thirty-two of his previous bouts with one drawn result. The challenger had relinquished the WBO crown to ensure his shot at Lewis. This looked to be an excellent encounter between the two men, both of who had excellent boxing abilities, but the contest proved to be a disappointment at Caesars Tahoe in Nevada, when Akinwande was disqualified for persistent holding in the fifth round of a bout set for the championship distance of twelve rounds. The contest never caught fire and Lewis gained little acclaim for this victory in a bout that was clearly not going to be listed in the top ten of the most exciting heavyweight title bouts of all time. This was, in essence, not a good or glorious start to Lewis's second reign. The styles of fighters are often badly matched, and this was one such occasion.

This was the fourth occasion a world heavyweight title fight had been decided by a disqualification since the introduction of the Marquess of Queensbury Rules. The previous three title fights were: Max Schmeling and Jack Sharkey on 12 June 1930, where Schmeling won the vacant crown in round four; when Joe Louis retained the championship in round seven against Buddy Baer on 23 May 1941; Evander Holyfield retaining the WBA version of the championship against Mike Tyson in round three on 28 June 1997.

The Lewis and Akinwande bout was the second occasion for two British heavyweights to contest a world heavyweight title fight against each other in the States. The first match took place on 11 January 1997 when Henry Akinwande defended the WBO crown against Scott Welch at The Nashville Arena, Tennessee, which saw the champion retain his title on points over twelve uninspiring rounds.

Andrew Golota

Lewis took to the ring to make his second defence of the championship, scheduled to take place once more on American turf. On 4 October 1997, Lewis this time put his crown on the line against Poland's Andrew Golota at Caesars Atlantic City Hotel and Casino. Golota had won twenty-eight of his thirty contests, but his two consecutive defeats had taken place in his last two bouts prior to facing Lewis.

Golota had lost his undefeated record against former undisputed world heavyweight king Riddick Bowe—twice by way of a disqualification, due to punches landing below the belt. The disqualifications took place in round seven on 11 July 1996, and round nine on 14 December 1996. On both occasions, the marauding Golota looked to be on his way to victory, but by landing his blows in forbidden territory it looked as though he had blown his chances of a crack at the championship. Despite the defeats, Golota landed a shot at the title. There was no mistaking the fact that Golota was a hard-punching foe—a man with fire in his belly and an unpredictability that made him very dangerous and not to be underestimated. Lewis and his team had done their homework, and were more than aware of what to expect.

Lewis needed to make a statement in this contest after his last two fights had failed to live up to expectations. Lewis needed not just to win but win well and put in a good performance that would enhance his reputation. Golota looked more than capable of making the contest World War Three if allowed to get into his stride and settle.

It is often considered that thirteen is an unlucky number. This was Lewis's thirteenth fight in America, and the figure proved to be anything but unlucky for the British fighter. On the night, Lewis really went to work, putting in a no-nonsense performance to produce a sensational victory that sent his credibility sky high. He had stopped his opponent in ninety-five seconds of the first round; it was a case of 'cometh the hour, cometh the man'. Golota did not know what hit him and, at the time of the stoppage, looked unsure as to whether he was in Poland or America.

The great Muhammad Ali once said of himself: 'I float like a butterfly and sting like a bee.' Lewis may not have been able to float with the grace of a butterfly, but in this bout he proved that he could most certainly sting like a bee. He had no intentions of travelling the full twelve-round route and preferred an early night. While the champion was favoured to retain his crown, no one could have foreseen such a quick and devastating win. When previously in the ring with Riddick Bowe, Golota had taken some solid blows from the former undisputed world champion and shrugged them off without being troubled by them—Bowe, make no mistake, packed a punch, and it had confirmed that Golota was a durable fighter. This fast win over Golota spoke volumes for the power that the Briton had in his arsenal, which gave him a psychological edge over Bowe, his former amateur victim.

Lewis had been ruthless in this defence of the championship; he had demolished a top-rated contender with contemptuous ease. When the fight was first signed, it looked as though Lewis would have a hard night's work ahead of him against a strong challenger, possibly being taken into the later rounds. Yet when Lewis came out of his corner it was not on a reconnaissance exercise to see what Golota had to offer, but on a seek-and-destroy mission.

This was a catastrophic defeat for Golota, who was found wanting badly on what was his big chance. The Polish contingent among the spectators must have been shocked by their man's quick capitulation since, in their hearts, they felt that Poland was going to see its first ever world heavyweight champion. If some critics were blasting Lewis's displays in previous bouts, they had no choice but to laud him highly for this night's work, which saw him cruise to his fifth win in the opening round. The champ was back on track and looking good.

For Golota, the future was somewhat different. He had to start the long process of rebuilding his career to get back among the leading contenders—a task that he accomplished as he was able to secure three more world title shots. On 17 April 2004, he challenged for the IBF version of the crown against defending champion Chris Byrd of America, coming close when the contest was declared a draw after twelve rounds. On 13 November 2004, he once again went for a world title, this time for the WBA championship against John Ruiz—a man who was the first Latino to hold a version of the title. Golota came up short, losing a twelve-round points decision to Ruiz. Golota went for the WBO version of the title, but again failed when stopped in the opening session by reigning champion Lamon Brewster of America on 21 May 2005.

Shannon Briggs

Lewis employed his fists once again in the USA when he took on American challenger Shannon Briggs on 28 March 1998 at the Broadwalk Convention Center, Atlantic City. Briggs had won thirty of his thirty-one bouts. Darroll Wilson had inflicted the sole defeat on 15 March 1996, which saw Briggs stopped in the third round. Since that setback, he had won his last five bouts in a row. In his last contest on 22 November 1997, Briggs had acquired his best win to date when he outpointed former two-time holder of the world heavyweight title, George Foreman, over twelve rounds in a closely contested bout. The fight with Foreman was billed for the lineal world heavyweight title.

To some this may have been a little confusing—yet another fighter claiming a version of the championship of the world. The explanation for calling the Foreman-Briggs meeting a world title bout was simple, and to some degree understandable, when considering the tradition of boxing. Foreman had won two versions of the championship from Michael Moorer in the ring on 5 November 1994 via a knockout in round ten. Foreman had later vacated the IBF crown since he was not prepared to meet the number-one contender, Axel Schulz of Germany. Foreman had previously defended against Schulz on 22 April 1995, winning a hard-fought contest that went to a twelve-round points decision. The WBA had previously stripped Foreman of their version of the title due to him not showing any signs of making a defence against Tony Tucker, their designated challenger. Foreman had lost his two titles without even throwing a punch. In the eyes of many, even though no longer recognised by a major sanctioning body, Foreman was still the champion until he was beaten inside the arena. So, since Briggs had done the deed, he claimed the crown. When the American met Lewis, he was not only holding the lineal title, he also had that good win over Foreman to his credit. Hence, Shannon's confidence of leaving the ring with the WBC championship belt strapped around his waist and adding to his lineal claim had to be sky high.

Briggs packed some dynamite in his fists and was not a fighter to be taken lightly—he was no patsy. This fact was proven when Lewis was caught and hurt by his challenger's explosive punches in the early stages of the contest; the champion had to take care since his challenger had won seventeen of his fights in the first round. Briggs was hunting his man down—a quick and concise win his intention. Lewis could not afford to expose his chin against his American opponent, who was more than capable of knocking out him out if he got careless. Briggs was nicknamed 'The Cannon' and, true to his moniker, he fired a number of broadsides at Lewis. The challenger was really going for it in no uncertain terms; he wanted that title and was not going to take any prisoners in his quest.

Some things in life are painfully obvious, and this was one such occasion; the fight would not last the distance. One would fall by knockout or stoppage before the final bell sounded to start round twelve. This was the American's big opportunity and he was not going to waste it.

Shannon proved to be a bigger threat than previously expected—certainly tougher than Lewis's last opponent, Golota. However, Lewis dug deep and showed he too had power in his punches coupled with a champion's heart; he had to gain Briggs's respect and keep him honest. Lewis duly came through the crises, using his ring-craft to stamp his authority on the bout and impressively stop Briggs in five rounds. Lewis attacked with a sustained assault, drilling his opponent with a series of blows that had 'the end' stamped indelibly on his gloves. Lewis knew he could not let his man off the hook and give him time to recover. He had to end the fight as quickly as he could and knock his man out. The American took three counts during the course of the contest before the referee intervened. Lewis was still the leader of the pack with the WBC belt firmly in his grasp—and was now also the lineal title holder.

The challenger may have lost the bout against Lewis, but this was not the end of Briggs on the big stage. He would later go on to capture the WBO version of the world heavyweight championship. Briggs was given the chance to once again challenge for a world crown on 4 November 2006, and took the most of his second opportunity by stopping holder Siarhei Liakhovich of Belarus in round twelve—a fact that puts even more value on Lewis's victory over Briggs.

Željko Mavrović

Before the year came to a close, Lewis put his crown on the line once again in America against Croatian Željko Mavrović on 26 September 1998. The challenger came into the ring with a 100 per cent record being undefeated in twenty-seven professional bouts. Mavrović had, to his credit, successfully defended the European heavyweight title on six occasions—two of said defences came against UK challengers. The first defeated Briton was Clifton Mitchell on 2 November 1996, who he stopped in round two; then future British and Commonwealth heavyweight king Julius Francis, who suffered the same fate in round eight on 15 February 1997.

While there was no doubt that Mavrović was worthy of a world title shot, it was notable that his CV lacked the names of any boxers considered even remotely world class. The only name that stood out was Italian Vincenzo Cantatore, who Mavrović defeated in his last bout before meeting Lewis on 18 October 1997. Mavrović looked good in stopping Cantatore in round four in what was a defence of his European championship. However, while Cantatore was a capable performer, he was not a top-flight heavyweight; he could not be described in any way as a world-beater. The victory by Mavrović was not one that would cause any concerns to the top fighters at the poundage.

At the Mohegan Sun Casino in Connecticut, Mavrović, a proud fighter, was to suffer his first loss in the paid ranks. Lewis predictably retained the championship on a twelve-round points decision. While Mavrović put in a good challenge, he was outboxed by Lewis, who clearly knew too much for him. Lewis had fought and beaten a higher calibre of fighter during the course of his career and this showed from the start. Few expected the championship to change hands, but a fighter can come of age in such a contest and spring a surprise—although on this night Lewis was simply at a much higher level than his opponent.

In defeat, Mavrović revealed a sturdy resistance to last the distance against a hard-punching champion. His chin appeared to have more granite than glass, which is a necessary attribute for a fighter aiming to go the top. The Croatian showed in his performance that he had a great deal to offer and could clearly figure in future lucrative, high-profile fights against other contenders in the division, perhaps even earn another world title shot in the fullness of time. However, despite the fact that the future ring prospects of Mavrović looked to be promising, the bout against Lewis surprisingly proved to be the last contest in his career.

On the other side of the Atlantic—on the same date at the Sports Village in Norwich, Norfolk, England—Herbie Hide, in his second reign as world heavyweight champion, made a second successful defence of his WBO crown by making short work of his challenger, easily stopping Germany's Willie Fischer in two rounds. This was the first time that two rival British world heavyweight champions had defended their titles on the same night. At that instant, it seemed that British heavyweight boxing was now at an all-time high.

Evander Holyfield (I)

Lewis was in action next against Evander Holyfield on 13 March 1999. Holyfield would be defending his WBA and IBF world titles against Lewis, who would be putting his WBC crown on the line. The winner would be considered the undisputed champion.

The task in front of Lewis was not an easy one. Holyfield had an outstanding record and had met a host of class fighters such as former world heavyweight kings Pinklon Thomas (WBC), who he defeated by a seven-round retirement on 9 December 1988, and Michael Dokes (WBA), who on 11 March 1989 was stopped in round ten when making a defence of his WBC Continental Americas heavyweight crown. Holyfield had well and truly won his spurs in the division and rightly earned his crack at the then reigning champion James Douglas.

On 25 October 1990, Holyfield was successful in his world title challenge, winning the heavyweight title belts from Douglas with consummate ease by way of a knockout in three rounds to become the undisputed champion. After defeating Douglas, Holyfield put his crown on the line against former undisputed heavyweight champion George Foreman, who he outpointed over twelve rounds on 19 April 1991. The second defence came against Bert Cooper on 23 November 1991, which proved to be a thrilling slugfest in which Holyfield retained his laurels by a stoppage in round seven. Former WBC and IBF king Larry Holmes was the third defence and also another victim on 19 June 1992—Holyfield outpointing him over twelve rounds.

Riddick Bowe was a fighter who would prove to be a thorn in Holyfield's side. The pair would provide the division with exciting match-ups. Holyfield and Bowe waged war on three occasions. The first time was on 13 November 1992 when Holyfield, the defending champion, lost his titles by way of a twelve-round points decision to Bowe. In their second meeting, Holyfield turned the tables in regaining the WBA and IBF crown on 6 November 1993 by winning a twelve-round points decision. Bowe had relinquished the WBC portion of the championship prior to meeting Holyfield. Holyfield and Bowe met again on 4 November 1995 when both were former world champions. On this occasion, Holyfield was stopped for the first time in his career in round eight. This setback did not deter Holyfield's fighting spirit since it was not too long before he had the gloves back on again to continue his trade.

Former WBO heavyweight king Michael Moorer proved to be a banana skin along the way when he outpointed Holyfield over twelve rounds to take the WBA and IBF crown on 22 April 1994. Moorer was a maker of boxing history having been the first southpaw-stance fighter to win a version of the world heavyweight title. Moorer achieved this feat by stopping Bert Cooper in round five on 15 May 1992 to capture the vacant WBO crown. Holyfield rebounded from his defeat to Moorer to conquer former WBO world heavyweight champion Ray Mercer on 20 May 1995 with a ten-round points decision.

Holyfield thus later returned to the ring on 10 May 1996 to log a decent win over former IBF world light-heavyweight and WBA cruiserweight king, Bobby Czyz, by a fifth-round retirement. Holyfield was later presented with another world title opportunity against the then WBA heavyweight king Mike Tyson. This was in no shape or form an opportunity gift wrapped in a gold ribbon. In many ways, the championship tilt looked to be a difficult mission beating Czyz who was a good fighter was one thing but taking on and defeating Tyson was something else. The bout with Tyson at this stage of his career seemed to be beyond Holyfield, who looked to be heading for a painful defeat. In some quarters, there were serious concerns about his well-being against the defending champion who gave no quarter in the ring and looked capable of walking through Holyfield. Against all the odds, Holyfield showed that his days as a world champion were far from over when he defeated Tyson on 9 November 1996 via an eleven-round stoppage to regain the WBA crown. A return contest between the two was duly arranged and it was thus wondered if Tyson would make amends for his setback against Holyfield in their second meeting and gain revenge. The meeting between the pair, which stirred up a great deal of interest, took place on 28 June 1997. Those expecting an all-out war were disappointed—Holyfield once again defeated Tyson, this time by a third-round disqualification.

On 8 November 1997, Holyfield met Michael Moorer in a unification bout. Holyfield was putting his WBA crown on the line against Moorer's IBF title. After Moorer had beaten Holyfield in their first meeting, he had experienced mixed fortunes in his career having lost the WBA and IBF crown in his first defence to former champion George Foreman by a knockout in round ten on 5 November 1994. Since the defeat to Foreman, Moorer had commendably fought his way back to the top and regained the IBF belt (which was at that time vacant) by outpointing Axel Schulz over twelve rounds on 22 June 1996. The contest with Holyfield would be Moorer's third defence of the crown in his second reign and he was thus fired up and once again ready to defeat Holyfield and retain his portion of the crown. There was a great deal for him to go for—defeating Holyfield would put him in line to do battle with Lewis in a big-money affair. However, not for the first time in his fistic career, Holyfield showed that he was not a fighter to be written off and gained his much sought-after revenge for the previous defeat when he forced Moorer to retire in round eight to add the IBF title to his WBA championship.

There was no doubt that Holyfield's record was a who's who of boxing, both at cruiserweight and heavyweight—you name him, Holyfield had fought him. It could be said, with justification, that Holyfield had mixed with a higher calibre of opposition than Lewis had prior to their meeting and, experience-wise, more than had the edge. Holyfield was in his third reign as a world heavyweight title holder and was also a former WBA, WBC, and IBF world cruiserweight champion. The American had a record of thirty-six wins with three defeats, had engaged in eleven world heavyweight titles bouts and six world cruiserweight championship contests. Holyfield was nicknamed 'The Real Deal', and this he most certainly was. It should be remembered that Holyfield was also a pretty smooth exponent of boxing in the amateur code, winning a bronze medal at the 1984 Los Angeles Olympic Games in the light-heavyweight division.

This was the man Lewis was up against; a true quality fighter, at home in the ring. When considering the fight history of Holyfield, one had to wonder if Lewis could produce anything in the ring that Holyfield had not seen before. Lewis knew that he had to be at his very best if he was to emerge victorious against such an excellent participant.

Once the bell sounded, the two men went about their task with relish. Both fighters were aware of how high the stakes were in their contest. Prior to the fight, Holyfield had predicted that he would knock Lewis out in three rounds—and therefore put a little unnecessary pressure on himself by doing so. To his credit, Holyfield tried to live up to his prediction by throwing a great deal of leather at his opponent, only to use a great deal of energy in doing so. Holyfield caught Lewis and stunned him in the stated session, but the Briton came back with his own brand of fire and was still there when the bell sounded to end the stanza.

The fight was full of action with both men giving and taking solid punches. Lewis could not afford to lose concentration and remained alert in every round. Holyfield was a constant danger, always looking to land the knockout. Lewis worked hard in each and every round—fighting a rival champion like Holyfield was never going to be easy. However, Lewis looked in control throughout the fight, making good use of his left jab.

At the end of the twelve-round bout it looked as if Lewis had done more than enough to secure the victory—but while he looked home and dry, surprisingly a draw was given. This, of course, meant that both fighters kept their respective version of the championship. It was obviously clear that a return had to take place between the two men. At the time, the decision was considered highly controversial: many were of the opinion that Lewis was a little hard done by. While this was a disappointment for Lewis, he took from the fight the knowledge that he had the beating of Holyfield well within his grasp and, if a return was to be made, he would emerge the winner.

Evander Holyfield (II)

A return fight between Lewis and Holyfield took place on 13 November 1999 at the Thomas and Mack Centre in New York. It was pleasing that the pair were to meet again without any undue delay. Those who knew their boxing felt that this time Lewis would defeat Holyfield even more clearly than before to ensure that he got the rightful decision. Thus, the British fighter entered the ring as favourite, although the American was not one anyone could confidently bet against. He was more than capable of lifting his game and pulling off a surprise when up against it. Holyfield was one dangerous fighter, a man who could dig deep into his fighting soul and produce something a little special to find a solution to overcome the problem in front of him.

In their rematch, Lewis and Holyfield fought an intelligent fight, both showing respect for each other during the heat of battle, attempting not to make any mistakes and give the other any kind of advantage. At that moment in time, the spectators in attendance sat in their seats in the knowledge that they were watching the best two fighters in the division plying their trade. The two boxers used their jabs, with Lewis getting the better of the exchanges. It was, in a sense, a chess match within a boxing ring, each man using his brain along with his fists. The contest was not one that kept spectators on the edge of their seats in suspense—not a blast-them-out, rip-snorting encounter in the style of the historic 'Thrilla in Manila' world title bout that had taken place on 1 October 1975. On that particular occasion, defending champion Muhammad Ali and challenger Joe Frazier met in what is described as one of the greatest championship fights in the division. Both men pushed each other to the very limit of their endurance, fighting way beyond the call of duty until Frazier's corner retired him at the end of round fourteen. However, to be fair, very few world championship bouts can match the standard of that meeting between two fantastic fighters. The Lewis and Holyfield battle was an interesting affair that held the attention and, in turn, showcased the various skillsets both boxers had at their disposal. Both fighters landed with solid shots, hoping to finish the fight long before the bell signalled the end of the contest. It was not easy for Lewis, but then no one expected a bout with Holyfield to be a walkover. The American always dug deep and then dug still deeper to find that little extra in his attempt to achieve victory. The bout once again went the full distance of twelve rounds, with Lewis this time being given the point's decision.

The job was done and the mission accomplished; Lewis was the holder of the WBC, WBA, IBF, and the IBO crowns. The British fighter was the undisputed world heavyweight champion and the first UK-born fighter to be acclaimed as such since Bob Fitzsimmons, who reigned from 1897–1899. It was a massive boost for boxing to once again have a unified world champion. Sadly, this situation did not last for long. The Briton later relinquished the WBA portion of the championship rather than defend it against the organisation's designated challenger John Ruiz. This opened the door for Holyfield to once again fight for a version of the world heavyweight title.

Holyfield thus contested the vacant crown with Ruiz on 12 August 2000 and amazingly won a twelve-round points decision to claim the crown. In so doing, Holyfield became the first man to win a version of the championship on four separate occasions, adding even more to his splendid ring legacy and thus making the win by Lewis look even greater.

Michael Grant

Lewis stepped into the ring at Madison Square Gardens in New York on 29 April 2000 to defend the WBC, IBF, and IBO versions of the title against American contender Michael Grant, who was undefeated in thirty-one bouts. Some fight experts felt that Grant, an ex-basketball player, had the skillset to dethrone the champion and return the titles to the USA. At first glance, Grant really did look to have all the necessary requirements to become a champion, and he was duly being groomed as the new star in the heavyweight boxing division.

Many of those pundits who felt that the battler from the USA was a king-in-waiting and had the beating of the British title holder should have taken notice of his bout before meeting Lewis. Grant had successfully defended his NABF heavyweight crown (in a contest that had also doubled as a WBC eliminator against Andrew Golota) on 20 November 1999 by a stoppage in round ten. The win was not a walk in the park for Grant—he certainly did not have time to stop and smell the roses along the way. He took two counts in the first round before fighting his way to victory. The knockdowns were not a good sign and should have been a warning that his chances against Lewis may not be that good—although many will say, quite rightly, that Grant showed heart to get up and win, which in turn showed the character and attributes of a future champion. Also, it has to be said that Golota was not an easy task, since he was not a burned-out fighter boxing just for the dollars; he felt that he had something to offer. However, a man considered to be a potential world champion like Grant should have handled his opponent more easily. Golota had, of course, failed in his bid to win the world crown on 4 October 1997 when halted by Lewis in the first round. Since that defeat, Golota had strung together six victories, putting himself back into contention prior to his bout with Grant.

The Briton once again proved his supremacy in the division, showing America and the world that he was not ready to step down from his throne. The defence turned out to be an easy one with Grant taking three counts in the first round after making an aggressive start. Lewis, who put his punches together impressively, accomplished the victory with a second-round knockout without having to dig too deep into his boxing bag of tricks. Lewis hardly worked up a sweat during the contest. The Briton was the supreme power in the division; a true king worthy of the titles he held. For Grant, he would have a difficult, if not impossible, task attempting to re-establish himself as a serious contender for the championship after such a crushing defeat.

On the same bill, Lewis's stablemate, Paul Ingle, made it a double world title success for Britain when, in defence of his IBF featherweight crown, he defeated former WBA world bantamweight and WBO super-bantamweight king Junior Jones, stopping the American challenger in the eleventh round of an exciting contest. Ingle also picked up the IBO version of the championship, which Jones was defending at the time. Scotland's future two-time WBO world featherweight champion, Scott Harrison, outscored former WBC world super-bantamweight and IBF world super-featherweight king Tracy Harris Patterson over ten rounds. Tracy was the adopted son of former two-time world heavyweight champion Floyd Patterson.

Frans Botha

South African Frans Botha was next on the agenda on 15 July 2000 at the New London Arena, Millwall, London. This was the first time that Lewis had fought in England since 24 September 1994 when, on that ill-fated fight, he lost his world crown to Oliver McCall via a second-round stoppage. Lewis was confident that it would prove to be a successful home coming.

It was clear that Lewis's WBC, IBF, and IBO titles could not be safer even if they were locked in a vault in the Bank of England; he dominated the bout from the first bell. Botha had challenged unsuccessfully on two occasions for the IBF version of the crown. The first time, on 9 December 1995, was against Axel Schulz for the vacant crown. After being given the twelve-round points decision, the bout was declared a non-contest when the South African tested positive for an illegal substance. Botha's second attempt took place on 9 November 1996, and once again the IBF championship proved to be an elusive object when he was stopped in round twelve by the American holder, Michael Moorer.

On 16 January 1999, Botha gave former world heavyweight king Mike Tyson a run for his money before being knocked out in round five. The South African rebounded from this defeat when, on 7 August 1999, he fought a ten-round draw with future WBO king Shannon Briggs. Prior to his meeting with Lewis, Botha had dispatched opponent Steve Pannell on 8 January 2000 with a first-round stoppage to show that he still had some fuel left in the tank and was not running completely dry. On entering the ring to face Lewis, Botha had an excellent ring record of forty wins, two defeats, one draw, and one no contest. The fight CV suggested that the South African was not exactly a no-hoper and it was more than plausible to think that he just might find that something extra and give a good performance, especially as it appeared that this could very well be his last shot at a major version of the world title. As it happened, Botha fought once again for a world heavyweight title when, on 16 March 2002, he challenged the reigning WBO heavyweight king, Wladimir Klitschko. The bid ended in failure when he was stopped in the eighth round.

The last South African to hold a version of the world heavyweight title was Gerrie Coetzee, who reigned as WBA king from 23 September 1983 to 1 December 1984.

It is often said that it takes two to tango. It also takes two to fight, and despite his vast ring experience Botha had no answer to the ring skills of the British fighter when the contest got underway. Botha was outclassed from the start and was unable to get into the bout or land any blows of consequence to make a fight of it. The chance of the South African going the full twelve rounds looked remote. The defending champion was outclassing his opponent, delivering in style and almost putting his challenger on the deck in the first round. The second stanza brought no joy or a change in fortune as Botha was sent sprawling through the ropes by Lewis's fists whereupon the referee mercifully stopped the contest in Lewis's favour. The South African came to do his best, but Lewis was on top form and increasingly looked to be an unbeatable fighter at that moment in time. This contest proved to be the last time that Lewis was to fight in the UK.

Wladimir Klitschko

On 14 October 2000, Wladimir Klitschko of Ukraine—who in his previous contest had fought on the undercard of the Lewis and Botha world title fight in London, stopping American Monte Barrett in round seven—joined the list of possible candidates who could meet Lewis in a championship bout.

Klitschko challenged defending WBO champion Chris Byrd of America for his title and won a twelve-rounds points decision in Cologne, Germany. Klitschko had put in a confident performance to take the crown. Wladimir Klitschko was the younger brother of former WBO king Vitali, who had lost the title to Byrd on 1 April 2000 when he had to retire in round nine due to a torn rotator cuff, so there was an element of revenge for the Klitschko family, with honour having been restored by Wladimir Klitschko. Byrd had the dubious distinction on that occasion of being the first man to win the world heavyweight crown from a fighter, only to lose it again to his brother.

Wladimir Klitschko looked a good fighter, one who could make more than a significant impact on the division in the fullness of time. Klitschko also had excellent amateur credentials, having won a gold medal at the 1996 Olympic Games in Atlanta at the super-heavyweight poundage. Klitschko looked capable of giving Lewis an interesting night should the occasion ever arise. Such a promotion would pit two former Olympic super-heavyweight gold medal winners together (Lewis won gold in 1988) to contest the championship—a fact that would put a good commercial spin on the event. Something no doubt various boxing promoters were mulling over.

David Tua

It was a trip over the Atlantic to the Mandalay Bay Resort & Casino in Las Vegas for Lewis to once again put his titles on the line, this time against New Zealand's David Tua, who had an impressive log of thirty-seven victories and one defeat. The last fighter from New Zealand to challenge for the world heavyweight crown was Tom Heeney, who had failed in his attempt when stopped in round eleven by defending American champion Gene Tunney on 23 July 1928.

Tua did not look to have the boxing ability to rip the championship away from Lewis and become his country's first world title holder in the division. However, it had to be appreciated that he was not a pushover—not a man to submit without making a fight of it. Tua would slug it out to the very end, meaning he had to be approached with a certain amount of caution and respect. Among his victims were standout names such as future WBA world heavyweight champion, John Ruiz, who Tua knocked out in the first round on 15 March 1996 in a contest for the WBC International heavyweight title. Then, in the third defence of that championship on 5 April 1997, he defeated yet another future world heavyweight king, Oleg Maskaev (WBC), with a stoppage in round eleven. Then, in a contest for the USBA heavyweight crown and the IBF Inter-Continental heavyweight title, he put the skids under yet another future world heavyweight king, Hasim Rahman, stopping his man in round ten on 19 December 1998. Rahman later went on to capture the WBC, IBF, and IBO titles. Tua's only defeat had come when he was outpointed over twelve rounds by the then highly regarded Ike Ibeabuchi to lose his WBC International title. That loss, which took place on the 7 June 1997, was a setback, but it should be taken into consideration that Ibeabuchi was undefeated in sixteen bouts and was highly regarded at the time. Tua had also made his mark in the amateur ranks by winning the Olympic bronze medal at heavyweight in the 1992 games in Barcelona.

Lewis once again revealed his class on 11 November 2000, clearly outpointing his man over the twelve rounds to keep the titles in his grasp. Tua, as expected, did not surrender meekly. He showed vast degrees of determination, plus the vital ability to take a punch. Despite Tua's attributes during the contest, there was no doubting that Lewis was superior—he showed no vulnerability whatsoever. Lewis used his left jab to good effect in keeping his man at bay, mixed with a heavy right hand that landed frequently on target. It appeared that Lewis was still head and shoulders above the rest of the fighters in the division.

Hasim Rahman (I)

The next challenge for Lewis's WBC, IBF, and IBO titles came from American Hasim Rahman in South Africa at Carnival City, Brakpan, Gauteng, on 22 April 2001. The defence against Rahman, who was nicknamed the 'Rock', looked like a formality since the American was not considered to be the *crème de la crème* of heavyweight challengers. Lewis looked a class above his challenger, but it had to be said that the American was not a toothless tiger—he could bite and bite hard if allowed to do so.

Rahman had fought his way through the ranks to earn a record of thirty-four victories with two defeats. He had won various titles, such as the IBF Inter-Continental crown, the United States Boxing Association, and USA Maryland State heavyweight championship. On 20 May 2000, Rahman captured the lightly regarded WBU world heavyweight crown by stopping holder and future WBO world heavyweight champion Corrie Sanders in round seven. One of the two Rahman defeats that stood out like sore thumbs was a ten-round stoppage to David Tua on 19 December in 1998—a contest in which he lost his Inter-Continental and USBA heavyweight titles. Tua was the fighter who Lewis had outpointed in his last defence, a further fact that did not inspire confidence in Rahman's challenge. The American had also fallen short on 6 November 1999, when knocked out in round eight by the future WBC world heavyweight title holder, Oleg Maskaev of Russia. Rahman had a win over the former WBC heavyweight king, Trevor Berbick of Canada, who he had outpointed over ten rounds on 15 October 1996. This was a good and solid victory, but, as often is the case in these situations, Berbick was not the fighter he once was—simply a name brought in for Rahman that represented little, if any danger to the American. Clearly, there was little indication in the record to suggest that Rahman was in any shape or form a significant threat to Lewis's reign as heavyweight king.

Lewis had met and defeated far better fighters than Rahman had during his career. Common sense dictated that the British fighter would have little trouble with the American in their fistic duel. The general consensus was that Lewis was the man with the skills and know-how to claim another victory and defence well before round twelve was reached. If a defeat was waiting for Lewis along the way, it was not going to happen on this night against Rahman—bigger and more lucrative fights were on the agenda for Lewis.

However, nothing should be taken for granted inside a boxing ring. On this occasion, the division saw a new champion crowned when Rahman used his mitts to good effect and produced a shock by knocking out Lewis in five rounds. Rahman landed a terrific right hand to send the defending champion crashing down to the canvas, whereupon he failed to beat the count. When helped back to his corner, Lewis looked discombobulated, unable to believe what had just happened. In the new champion's corner, the celebrations were, as would be expected, more than just a little joyful. This was a massive blow to Lewis. Such was the unbelievable win by Rahman that one had to wonder upon seeing the bout if they had somehow slipped into a twilight zone—surely that was not Lewis hitting the canvas?

Of course, it was. Boxing has a history of upsets, and Rahman's victory over Lewis added to that very long list. Some shrewd boxing observers felt that Lewis did not give himself enough time to acclimatise to Johannesburg's high altitude, which is said to be approximately 5,200 feet above sea level. Lewis arrived in South Africa just two weeks prior to the contest after filming a boxing scene in the George Clooney film *Ocean's Eleven* (2001). Some even felt that Lewis had underrated his opponent and paid the price for taking him lightly, which seemed more than possible.

Whatever the reason, the rights or wrongs about the defeat, Lewis was now a former world champion for the second time in his career, and had the daunting task of digging deep and rebuilding his career. The Briton had fought his way back to the championship after the Oliver McCall two-round stoppage loss on 24 September 1994—the big question now to be answered was, would he be able to do so again?

Hasim Rahman (II)

The first time Lewis lost his title, he had to fight various opponents to earn his chance at regaining the championship. This time, Lewis was given an immediate return, without having to go through the arduous task of fighting any contenders for the opportunity. This was not due to the team behind Rahman being keen to meet Lewis again, far from it. Easier options were open to them and they were prepared to take them and cash in on the title. Business-wise, they could not be blamed for considering that route, but there was a return clause to meet Lewis, a fact that the new champion could not sidestep or avoid. Lewis wanted this return fight and was straining at the leash to face the American again. Lewis duly won a court case, forcing Rahman to honour the clause that had been in the fight contract; Lewis had won the first round simply in getting Rahman back inside the ring. Now it was game on.

The golden chance for Lewis to regain his titles took place on 17 November 2001 at the Mandalay Bay Resort and Casino in Las Vegas. This time, Rahman had the confidence of knowing he had beaten Lewis once, which gave him the edge in believing that he could do so again. There was always the chance that the Briton could be slipping and on the way out, the possibility that a long career in both the amateur and paid ranks had caught up with him and eroded his skills. Had Lewis gone to the well once too often, only to find that it had now run dry?

Any such thoughts were soon put to rest when Rahman found that he was facing a far different fighter from the one he had previously defeated.

Wisdom in life is a valuable asset, often only acquired after we have lived for some years, made mistakes, and duly learnt from them. Wisdom in the ring is an equally valuable asset for a fighter, one which is often obtained after taking part in a number of contests and learning by mistakes made along the way. Lewis was now a wiser man and a much wiser fighter. Rahman, the defending champion, was to face the real Lewis—a class fighter this time on his game 100 per cent; a man who was going to right a wrong and reclaim his property.

Lewis fought with passion and bossed the fight from the off. He boxed in a classy, intelligent way, picking his shots superbly and implacably. The British fighter looked for any openings in Rahman's defence and exploited them to the full, using his vast boxing repertoire to do so. This was Lewis the master, not the Lewis who had made errors the first time around.

The opening round of the contest had not been a good one for the defending champion; he was out-jabbed and finished the session with a cut above his left eye. When the chance presented itself, the Briton lowered the boom, knocking out his man in round four to take back the championship and avenge his previous defeat. All of the judges' scorecards had Lewis in front at the time of the finish, but this made little difference to the British fighter, who had provided his own judges and referee in the form of sheer punching power.

Lewis had looked as good as ever and, on this performance, far superior to rival title holders Wladimir Klitschko (WBO) and John Ruiz (WBA). More lucrative fights loomed ahead for the British fighter, who was still the main man in the division—Rahman regained the WBC crown later in his career. Prior to meeting Rahman in the return contest, Lewis had parted company from his manager Frank Maloney.

On the same fight card, two of Lewis's previous opponents met in a bout scheduled for ten rounds: former WBC world heavyweight king Oliver McCall, and WBO world heavyweight title holder Henry Akinwande. Since their respective contests against Lewis, McCall had taken part in eleven bouts, winning ten with one no contest. Akinwande had won eight of his bouts and looked capable of boxing his way to victory against his American opponent. However, McCall once again confirmed that he was not a man to undersell when he knocked out his opponent in round ten. McCall was now back in the mix, while Akinwande had to rebuild his career.

Mike Tyson

At the age of twenty years, four months, and twenty-three days, Mike Tyson had made history by becoming the youngest man to win a version of the world heavyweight title when he hammered defending WBC king Trevor Berbick to defeat in two rounds on 22 November 1986. Tyson later went on to unify the championship by defeating rivals James Smith (WBA) on points over twelve rounds on 7 March 1987, and then Tony Tucker (IBF) on 1 August 1987 also on points over the duration of twelve rounds.

Tyson was a force in the division, a real wrecking ball and destroyer of all who dared to confront him in the ring. Tyson had power in his punches and would take his opponents out if the chance presented itself, showing no mercy when doing so. No one was able to stand in his way. He seemed invincible—a force of nature and the most destructive man on the planet. Tyson was a truly frightening figure in the ring with no chinks in his armour.

Many boxing experts made the prediction that he would have a very long championship reign and would be ranked with the greats like Joe Louis, Muhammad Ali, Rocky Marciano, and Jack Dempsey. This prediction had looked good until he met fellow American James Douglas on 11 February 1990 in Tokyo, Japan—then it all went terribly wrong. Douglas did the unexpected by knocking out Tyson in ten rounds to win the titles, which to call a shock result would be putting it mildly. It was one of the greatest boxing upsets in years. Tyson was flying high at the time, but in boxing the higher the flight, the further the fall when defeated. A bet on Douglas prior to the fight would have won a bundle.

Tyson and Douglas did not meet again in the ring in the years that followed. In fact, the fortunes of Douglas changed dramatically after beating Tyson when he lost the championship on 25 October 1990 in his first defence—knocked out in three rounds by the challenger, Evander Holyfield, at the Mirage Hotel & Casino in Las Vegas. While Holyfield was a good fighter—no argument about that—watching the bout did beg the question: where did the man who defeated Tyson go?

Following his loss to Douglas, Tyson returned to his winning ways and fought back into championship contention, regaining both the WBC and WBA titles on separate occasions. Tyson stopped Britain's WBC king Frank Bruno in three rounds on 16 March 1996 at the MGM Grand in Las Vegas, only to later relinquish the championship. Then, on 7 September 1996, he stopped defending WBA king Bruce Seldon in the first round at the MGM Grand to regain the WBA crown. Tyson looked back to his old destructive self and appeared to be on target to once again to be a major force in the division. Sunny days seemed ahead, yet storm clouds were slowly gathering.

Evander Holyfield was the next man to climb into the ring to confront the fearsome Tyson on 9 November 1996. While Holyfield was a fine opponent who knew his trade, many feared he would face certain defeat. However, boxing presented yet another shock to the sporting world. At the MGM Grand, the championship changed hands after a hard-hitting encounter between the two fighters when Tyson surprisingly lost the WBA title in his first defence. On the night, Holyfield really fancied the job and matched the champion blow by blow, stopping his opponent in round eleven.

A return contest between Holyfield and Tyson was a must and the pair got together once again at the MGM Grand on 28 June 1997. It was a bout that looked likely to be an all-out war that would produce some spectacular moments of action. Many would not have been too surprised if, on this occasion, Tyson found his form to defeat Holyfield and took back the WBA crown. However, the fight took an unusual and shocking turn to end in a way no one could have predicted. Tyson, seemingly taking the notion of a 'hungry' fighter to the extreme, was disqualified in round three for biting Holyfield's ears. It was abundantly clear that Tyson, despite the fact that he had impressively fought his way back to championship status with his victories over Bruno and Seldon, was no longer the same fighter he had once been before his first defeat to James Douglas.

Tyson entered the ring to challenge Lewis on 8 June 2002 at the Pyramid, Memphis, Tennessee, for the WBC, IBF, and IBO championship. His record was a very commendable forty-nine wins, three defeats, and two bouts ruled a non-contest. Since his defeat to Holyfield, Tyson had fought on six occasions, racking up four victories with two respective bouts being ruled a non-contest.

The Lewis and Tyson match-up was a must-see for fight fans. However, it was a contest which was long overdue—one that should have taken place two to three years earlier. The George Foreman and Muhammad Ali world heavyweight contest that had taken took place in Zaire—now The Democratic Republic of the Congo—on 30 October 1974 was dubbed 'The Rumble in the Jungle'. The Muhammad Ali and Joe Frazier world title bout that put the two fighters together for a third time took place on 1 October 1975 in the Philippines was dubbed the 'Thrilla in Manila'. 'Better Late than Never' might have been an appropriate billing for the Lewis and Tyson showdown.

The animosity between the two fighters showed at a pre-fight press conference. The meeting proved to be an ugly, bad-tempered affair, ending in a brawl that forced the security men on hand to intervene and separate Lewis and Tyson from one another. During the melee, it was reported that Tyson had bitten Lewis on the leg. This attracted a good deal of media attention that filled the sports pages of many newspapers and television channels across the world. The spectacle was not exactly a good advertisement for the sport, but it is often said that there is no such thing as bad publicity—although sometimes one has to wonder if that is true. Nonetheless, there was no doubting the fact that the flare-up between the two did indeed add a degree of spice to their scheduled meeting in the ring.

It would be fair to say that Tyson's best days were in the past. During a contest, a boxer is always advised to keep off the ropes, but that was where Tyson's career had found itself. Nevertheless, he was still a dangerous fighter and could not be viewed as an easy night's work as the intense fire of a warrior still burned brightly within his soul. This factor helped to produce a degree of both tension and drama to the proceedings. The American knew that the bout with Lewis could well be his last chance at a world crown, and that defeat would signal the end of his career in the big league. It was a case of all or nothing for Tyson, a boom or bust affair, which made him a dangerous man.

Lewis would be the fourth Olympic gold medallist Tyson had fought in a professional ring. In defence of his WBC, WBA, and IBF titles on 16 October 1987, Tyson had stopped Tyrell Biggs (1984 Los Angeles super-heavyweight) in round seven. In a further defence of the titles, he knocked out Michael Spinks (1976 Montreal middleweight) in the opening round on 27 June 1988. Then, a former world champion Tyson met Henry Tillman (1984 Los Angeles heavyweight) on 16 June 1990, which resulted in another inside-the-distance victory with Tillman knocked out in the first round. Would Tyson add another Olympian gold medallist to his list of victims?

Prior to the start of the contest, security men in yellow shirts formed a line across the ring to ensure that the two fighters did not indulge before the bell sounded. There was even the unusual spectacle of two ring announcers, Jimmy Lennon and Michael Buffer, inside the square war zone, both of whom carried out their duties with impeccable style. Among the spectators were celebrities Samuel L. Jackson, Denzel Washington, Wesley Snipes, Kevin Bacon, and the future President of the USA, Donald J. Trump.

Once the fight began, Tyson went quickly after his man, looking for the pay-off punch. Lewis responded by landing solid blows of his own. It soon became apparent that Lewis was the superior fighter, a man who was taking stock of the threat in front of him and carefully watching his challenger's every move in order to take steady control of the contest. The American, however, continued to go after his foe without any form of hesitation, looking for the blow that would win the championship, turn his career around, and resuscitate his ring life. Lewis was unfazed by his ever-advancing challenger and was able to parry his blows and counter with his own damaging punches. Tyson had no option but to eat the jabs that Lewis threw in his direction. Boxing is often called the 'noble art'; if the sport is truly an art form, then on that day Lewis was the fight games' answer to Rembrandt, his gloves the substitute for the artist's paint brush and easel. His performance was producing a masterpiece on canvas, albeit one stained with blood rather than paint.

Tyson fought an uphill battle and was unable to turn the fight in his favour. He struggled to avoid or block the leather that Lewis threw in his direction with increasing persistency and venom. In round four, Lewis was deducted a point for pushing Tyson over. However, this proved to be just a slight setback as the British fighter dominated and bossed the bout in such a way that it was obvious the fight would not go the full distance. Tyson, who looked a battle-weary fighter with blood flowing from his nose and cuts over both eyes, was bravely taking punishment, but even his tough exterior could only take so much. Finally, in round eight, Lewis closed the show when he knocked out the American with a right hand to the jaw. Moments before Lewis landed the blow to finish the fight, Tyson had taken a left uppercut, which badly stunned him. This resulted in him dipping down and the referee giving him an eight count.

The much-anticipated fight between the two was over. It really did mark the end for Tyson, since his aura of invincibility had been completely stripped from him in violent fashion. The fear that intimidated his opposition before the bell had sounded to start the contest was now just a thing of the past. Often after a fight of such magnitude, there is speculation that a return bout might be in the making in the future. Such was the dominance of Lewis's victory over Tyson that there was no such speculation. The era of Mike Tyson was over.

After the Lewis contest, it might have been prudent for Tyson to bid goodbye to the sport. Sadly, he fought on, perhaps clinging to the hope that he might be able to turn back the clock and produce the fire and desire of old. Every fighter feels that he has one more good fight left in him, and sadly that feeling is often far from the truth. Tyson hence made what looked like a promising return on 22 February 2003, wasting no time in disposing of fellow American Clifford Etienne by knocking him out in the opening round. The contest took place at the Pyramid in Memphis, the venue where he met with defeat against Lewis. Then, on 30 July 2004, he met with disaster when former British and Commonwealth heavyweight champion Danny Williams ventured to the USA and knocked him out in the fourth round at the Freedom Hall State Fairground in Louisville, Kentucky. While Williams was a decent fighter at British and European level, few would have fancied his chances against the Tyson of old. The former world champion was falling further and further from the pinnacle he once held in the sport. The downwards spiral continued for Tyson when, on 11 June 2005, Ireland's Kevin McBride surprisingly stopped him in round six at the MCI Center in Washington, District State of Columbia. After this, Tyson wisely bowed out from the sport. There was nowhere else for him to go, as he had run out of road and options. Tyson's career inside the ring had clearly come to an end and his glory days were over. It would have been a sad sight had Tyson continued only to be a stepping stone for younger fighters on the way up.

For Lewis, the situation after his victory over Tyson was vastly different. It appeared that the world was his oyster. Lewis looked to have a career set to last for at least another two to three years. The Briton had fought all the viable contenders around and, at that moment in time, he looked untouchable in the ring. Lewis reigned supreme and could most certainly make more successful title defences without any problems should he still have the motivation to continue his trade. Motivation was now the keyword since it is a vital element that every sportsman has to possess in their make-up—and something that can evaporate with the passing of time.

After his win over Tyson, Lewis's legacy was more than secured. There was little else for him to prove. In the cold light of day, legacy is an important factor in a champion's career. Among the new crop of challengers for his title, there seemed few, if any, who represented a serious threat to Lewis and his reign, such was his domination over the division. Under these circumstances, it seemed more than likely that Lewis would put the gloves on once again, not just to keep his hands warm, but to fight on and notch up a few more successful defences. The defences would add to his already impressive record and bank balance. The prospect of more lucrative fights in the works made it impossible to walk away from the sport. That is always the temptation for champions—it is not easy to say goodbye when large chunks of cash are on offer to take on what looks like an easy defence, and who can blame them? After years of torturing their bodies in the gym, making sacrifices and taking hard knocks to get to where they are, they deserve every penny and reward they make from a championship. They work hard to obtain the crown, and to surrender it freely without a defence appears to be a foolish move financially. After all, one does not close down a gold mine when it is still producing gold. However, while that view makes good sense on an economic front, it has often proven to be a recipe for disaster for many of the fighters who have graced the prize ring. It should also be considered that it is not always the lure of money that keeps a boxer fighting inside the ring. Indeed, it is often a way of life for them, one they have had for a number of years and one that they find difficult to turn their back on and say goodbye to. This may be a concept that many fail to understand, especially those who have never been in the ring. It is not easy for retired fighters to adjust to a normal, everyday life once they have decided to hang up the gloves. This malaise affects not just champions, but often boxers on other levels too.

The pages of boxing history books are full of champions—and indeed, highly-ranked fighters—who have taken that one fight too many for one reason or another; those who have failed to take heed of the warning signs in their performances that clearly suggest the end is near. Sadly to say, far too many men who once ruled the world have gone on much longer than they should have, losing to opponents who would not have been able to lay a glove on them when in their prime years. It was to be hoped that Lewis would not fall into that trap and follow that well-trodden destructive path, but would know when the moment was right to call time on his career. Interestingly, only two world heavyweight champions had quit at the top while still holding the title at that time: Gene Tunney, who reigned from 1926–1928; and Rocky Marciano, who ruled the division from 1952–1956. Gladly, they did not make any ill-fated comebacks to the ring at a later date. They retired and stayed retired.

Roy Jones Jnr

On 1 March 2003, American Roy Jones Jnr won his fourth world title when, at the Thomas & Mack Center in Las Vegas, he captured the WBA version of the world heavyweight championship by outpointing holder John Ruiz over twelve rounds. The new WBA king now had a record of forty-eight victories and just one defeat.

Jones Jnr was also a former undisputed world light-heavyweight king, IBF middleweight, and IBF super-middleweight champion—he was regarded as something special. An exceptionally gifted ring operator, he had the habit of stunning the world of boxing with his outstanding exploits inside the ring—a man who was fated to be inducted into the International Hall of Fame in the future such were his performances and achievements. Jones Jnr was regarded as a modern-day great by many observers who applauded his work, some even stating that he was the best they had ever seen inside the ring. That was some accolade when considering some of the past greats who had fought in the ring over the years. It was also notable that Jones Jnr was the first former world middleweight champion since English-born Bob Fitzsimmons (who reigned in that division from 1891–1895) to win a version of the world heavyweight crown.

The speculation was underway that a Lewis–Jones Jnr heavyweight battle would be an attraction that would capture the imagination of the sporting public. Would the phenomenal Jones Jnr be able to add to his ever-growing greatness and topple Lewis in a unification fight? Would the Briton be one step too far? Would Lewis have the necessary kryptonite in his gloves to halt the American in his tracks? At that moment in time, Jones Jnr appeared to be the boxing version of Superman. In boxing, it is often said that a good 'big un' will always beat a good 'little un'; this favoured Lewis, but Jones Jnr was not just a good 'little un'—he was an exceptional 'little un', which made the topic even more fascinating. The fight, or the talk of a projected fight between the two, threw up a series of ifs and buts that made it a good conversation piece among fans. Such a meeting between the two men looked to be a massive promotion and a promising match-up, one guaranteed to pull in the big bucks in the USA and also have mass worldwide appeal.

However, all the speculation came to nothing, since the contest did not materialise. Jones Jnr later vacated the throne of WBA heavyweight champion and returned to the light-heavyweight division.

Corrie Sanders

On 8 March 2003, another possible candidate to fight Lewis arrived on the scene. Corrie Sanders of South Africa stepped into the ring at the Preussag Arena in Hannover, Germany, to challenge WBO king Wladimir Klitschko for the title. The champion from the Ukraine was making the sixth defence of the title that he had taken from American Chris Byrd on 14 October 2000 by way of a twelve-round points decision. It was felt that Klitschko would make another successful defence of his title against his latest challenger. Truth be told few, if any, gave Sanders a chance of leaving Germany with the championship belt packed in his suitcase.

Record-wise, there was not a great deal between the two going into the contest. Klitschko had participated in forty-one bouts with one defeat and Sanders had engaged in forty with two defeats. The champion had the edge in their duel since he had shared the ring with a higher calibre of opponent than his South African challenger and was considered to be the better technician of the two. However, once again, the unexpected happened inside the square ring. Sanders lived up to his nickname, 'The Sniper', by finding his range early to unload on his target, finding a way through the defences of the champion. The South African produced the powerful punches to tear the crown from the head of Klitschko, pulling off a surprising and sensational victory by stopping the defending title holder in impressive fashion in round two to make the ringside judges redundant.

Sanders had floored the defending champion twice in the first round and looked as if he might just finish it in that stanza before the bell rang to stop the action. In the following session, the challenger came out of his corner looking for the finish, putting Klitschko on the canvas twice more before the referee stepped in to call a halt to the contest. In doing so, Sanders became the second South African fighter to win a version of the championship—Gerrie Coetzee was the first. Sanders also became the third boxer with the southpaw stance to hold a version of the crown, the first two being American's Michael Moorer and Chris Byrd. Sanders looked like he would hold the championship for some time, but he later relinquished the crown without making a defence.

Vitali Klitschko

After his victory over Mike Tyson, Lewis spent a considerable time away from the ring and many wondered if he would fight again. It was considered that, after the high of defeating Tyson, the Briton had achieved everything he could in the sport. There was no one left for Lewis to conquer since he had cleaned up the division, proving that he was the best of his time.

However, any rumours of a Lewis retirement were quickly laid to rest when his return to the ring was announced. The next defence for Lewis was going to take place on 21 June 2003, one year and thirteen days after his last ring outing against Mike Tyson. The challenger was going to be Kirk Johnson of Canada—a good fighter, but hardly a challenger to get fans excited. The statistics of Johnson's record made good reading: he had taken part in thirty-six fights with one defeat and one draw. The loss came in a challenge for the WBA world crown on 27 July 2002 against holder John Ruiz by way of a disqualification in round ten for landing a low blow in a contest that was not a barn burner or a fight to get the pulse racing. Johnson's performance against Ruiz in no way suggested that he had any kind of chance of lifting a world title on his second attempt against Lewis. The drawn result on Johnson's CV had taken place on 8 December 1998 against former IBF world cruiserweight king Alfred Cole in a ten-round contest. In a return bout on 20 March 1999, Johnson took a ten-round points verdict over Cole. The Canadian had won the PAPA heavyweight title on 7 October 2000, knocking-out future WBC world heavyweight king Oleg Maskaev of Russia in round four. On 15 March 2003, he had won the WBO Inter-continental heavyweight bauble by stopping American holder Lou Savarese in four rounds.

Nonetheless, any speculation about the chances of Johnson against Lewis proved pointless. Johnson was unable to meet the champion for the title due to a tear to his pectoral muscle. Only the IBO crown would have been on the line in this instance anyway, since the WBC would not sanction the defence against Johnson. Lewis no longer held the IBF belt, having previously relinquished the trinket rather than meet Chris Byrd, the IBF's number one contender.

Ultimately, Ukrainian Vitali Klitschko ('Dr Iron Fist'), who had been scheduled to fight American Cedric Boswell on the undercard of the proposed Lewis and Johnson bout, was offered the opportunity to step up and meet Lewis. This was a golden chance that he gladly accepted with both gloved hands. Klitschko, the older brother of Wladimir Klitschko, was a former WBO world champion and a former two-time holder of the European title with an impressive professional record of 32 wins and just the sole defeat. That setback came at the hands of American Chris Byrd on 1 April 2000, when retiring in round nine due to a shoulder injury, reportedly a torn rotator cuff, which resulted in the loss of his WBO crown. The bout against Byrd had been Klitschko's third defence of the championship, which he had won in dramatic fashion by knocking out defending champion Herbie Hide of Britain in two sensational rounds on 26 June 1999. The bout that took place at the New London Arena, Millwall, England, was something of a surprise since many had favoured Hide to win the bout and retain the title. However, on the night, the Ukraine fighter blasted out Hide with ease and looked a dangerous proposition for any fighter in the division.

Based on past performances in the ring, Klitschko was not going to be a pushover and certainly not a man who would be defeated without making his presence felt. Also, it could be said that he was a better challenger than the original choice of Johnson. Klitschko was determined to prove that he was not just a substitute challenger stepping in to fill the void, but a warrior who intended to prove his worth and make the most of his unexpected opportunity to defeat Lewis and once again wear a world crown.

The title bout now involved both the WBC and IBO versions of the championship. The WBC clearly felt that Klitschko was an acceptable challenger, since he reportedly held the number one ranking with them, and they therefore agreed to sanction the Lewis defence against Klitschko. Whatever the sanctioning bodies said, be it for a belt or no belt, Lewis was the champion—the main man and the rightful king of the division. To be number one and accepted as the true title holder meant beating him inside the ring. There was no getting away from that fact.

The Lewis and Klitschko bout was to take place at the Staples Centre in Los Angeles and would be a history maker since it was the heaviest world heavyweight title bout to date. Lewis scaled a reported 18 st 4 lb and Klitschko 17 st 10 lb. With this fact in mind, those sitting at the ringside must have been a little nervous, hopeful that neither one of the participants would be knocked out of the ring and onto their lap during the bout. The unlucky ones would certainly require medical assistance if such an event took place.

There was much anticipation about the contest since this was the first world heavyweight championship bout to be staged in Los Angeles since reigning title holder Floyd Patterson stopped challenger Roy Harris by a twelve-round retirement at Wrigley Field on 18 August 1958. It was felt by some that after destroying Tyson, Lewis would despatch Klitschko without too much hardship, since the Ukrainian did not appear to have the versatility to cause the defending title holder any undue problems. Whatever Klitschko brought into the ring, Lewis would have the experience to cope with it.

Once the bout started Klitschko showed confidence, producing a strong challenge to give the WBC and IBO champion a torrid time. Klitschko made his intentions known from the off, delivering an impressive array of blows against the title holder. The bout quickly developed into a slugfest with the two juggernauts freely landing with damaging punches. The two men threw everything at each other and it was turning out to be an exciting fight, better perhaps than many might have have anticipated previously. There were moments when it looked as if Lewis, now aged thirty-seven years, nine months and nineteen days, was heading for defeat against the younger Klitschko, who was aged thirty-one years, eleven months and two days. It now looked as if Lewis would have been wiser to have made Tyson his last fight.

The last occasion on which a world heavyweight title was contested on this date was seventy-one years ago when the then defending champion, Max Schmeling, lost his crown to challenger Jack Sharkey on a fifteen-round points decision at the MSG Bowl, Queens, New York. It had to be wondered if history was going to repeat itself and Lewis, like Schmeling, was going to relinquish his championship to the challenger. However, Lewis hung in and met his challenger head-on, having to rely upon his vast experience. Both fighters were in the fight business and they were carrying it out with the utmost efficiently.

For Lewis, the fight was a test not just of his physical strength, but also for his mental resolve. How much punishment would Lewis endure to keep the title in his grasp? Had his ambition dissolved with the passing of time at the top? Was the hunger gone? Was the championship about to leave Britain for Ukraine? There were so many questions to be asked and answered before the night was over.

The two men waged war on each other, landing punch for punch, looking for the blow that would finalise the contest once and for all—no quarter was given. It was rough, tough, and brutal inside the ring; not a fight for the faint-hearted. The pace was hectic and neither was willing to surrender, even though in a fight of such punishment the canvas beneath the fighters' feet looked a warm and welcoming place to rest—a place of sanctuary from the hell they were going through. All they had to do was sink to one knee, get counted out by the referee, and then it would all be over. Nonetheless, both challenger and champion were not looking for an easy way out; they were fighters to the bitter end. It was not just the titles that were now at stake but honour and pride. Lewis had worked long and hard to become champion and had the benefit of seventeen world title bouts behind him—defeat was not an option he was willing to accept, nor a road he was prepared to walk down. If Klitschko wanted the crown, he would have to bite down on his gum shield and find yet another level or two in his attempts to take it.

It is often said that boxing is the hardest game. You would have to agree it is the hardest, but perhaps disagree about it being a game. Boxing is no game: it is a serious occupation fraught with pain and danger.

During the course of this bitter battle, the British 'Lion' roared and turned the fight around when he landed a solid blow that badly cut Klitschko over his left eye in the third stanza. The wound was a setback for the challenger. Without a doubt it was going to hinder his chances of a victory unless he could produce something special.

As expected, the cut worsened as the contest progressed, with blood running freely down Klitschko's face like a crimson river. The challenger ignored the claret and continued to go forwards, frequently finding the champion with his accurate blows. Lewis was also showing the signs of battle with a swelling starting to develop under his left eye. In round four, both men tumbled together on to the canvas during the battle, exhaustion setting in. The wound over Klitschko's left eye looked a nasty, bloody mess and was clearly a concern in the Ukrainian's corner and a major factor suggesting to all in attendance that the fight would not go on for too much longer. Had it not been a championship contest, the fight would have surely been halted sooner. Knowing that the sands of time, along with his chances of victory, were running out, Klitschko tried desperately to connect with a winning blow during round six, but it was to no avail.

To no one's surprise, the contest was halted at the end of round six on the advice of Dr Paul Wallace due to the damage to the challenger's eye. In addition, a further cut under Klitschko's left eye added to his woes. The stoppage saw Lewis retain his title after an unexpectedly difficult fight. The ending between the two gladiators was inconclusive and Klitschko was far from happy about the contest having been stopped at that stage. He wanted to fight on, but there was no doubt that the stoppage was correct and had the fight gone on the damage would have proven to be more severe.

The Ukrainian clearly felt that he had the beating of Lewis and asked him in the ring for a return. When the fight was stopped, all three of the official score cards, which were presented from the ringside judges after the fight, had Klitschko ahead on points. Lewis was adamant, however, that, even without the cut eye stoppage, he would have punched his way to victory. The challenger was a brave man and had the look of a fighter who would come again.

Lewis knew at the end of the contest that he had been in a serious fight. Both men must have felt the pain of conflict within their aching bodies for weeks after their meeting. It appeared that a return between the two was inevitable; a second meeting would certainly be a box office money spinner that would have the turnstiles ticking over and working overtime with both boxers seeing their bank balance substantiality improved. Considering the battle Klitschko had given Lewis in their first duel, the outcome of a second meeting would surely be an even, uncertain affair—it was certainly a return the public wanted to see. Klitschko had always been known as a good fighter, but his stock on the boxing market had now risen after his excellent and unexpectedly high-octane performance against Lewis. It was now felt that the Ukrainian, who came away from the contest highly praised by all who witnessed the world title bout, was more than just a good fighter. He was, in fact, a little special.

Much to the disappointment of Klitschko and many fight fans, the two boxers did not cross gloves again. There was a degree of speculation over the months that followed about a second meeting, but after some consideration, Lewis decided to retire from the sport that he had served so well, announcing his retirement on 6 February 2004.

Some felt that Lewis could have continued a little longer and that his retirement was premature—but was it? Many boxers have sadly gone on for far too long. Lewis was not going to add his name to the list of fighters who did not know when to say *adios*. The British fighter had thought it through and decided it was time to quit. He had made an intelligent decision; Lewis had nothing to prove and had served the sport with pride and dignity. Lewis was leaving boxing on his own terms while on top and still a reigning world champion, which in truth is the ideal way to say goodbye.

Looking at his career, it is clear that Lewis is a man destined to be ranked among the greats of the division in the fullness of time—of that there can be no argument. Lewis fought the best heavyweights during his time in the professional ring, which more than strengthens his claim to be ranked with the top men.

While not having held the WBO version of the crown, Lewis was considered to be the undisputed champion of the division during his reign. The Briton had fought forty-four professional contests, winning forty-one (thirty-four inside-the-distance knockouts, stoppages or disqualifications), losing two, and drawing one—both loses and the draw were avenged in return bouts. Lewis had fought fourteen men who, at one time or another, had held versions of a world championships: Ossie Ocasio (WBA cruiserweight); Mike Weaver (WBA heavyweight); Glen McCrory (IBF cruiserweight); Tony Tucker (IBF heavyweight); Frank Bruno (WBC heavyweight); Oliver McCall (WBC heavyweight); Tommy Morrison (WBO heavyweight); Ray Mercer (WBO heavyweight); Henry Akinwande (WBO heavyweight); Shannon Briggs (WBO heavyweight); Evander Holyfield (undisputed heavyweight); Hasim Rahman (WBC heavyweight); Mike Tyson (undisputed heavyweight); and Vitali Klitschko (WBC and WBO heavyweight). Frans Botha is not included in this list, since his victory over Axel Schulz for the vacant IBF world heavyweight title on 9 December 1995 was later declared a no contest when he failed a drug test.

Lewis, like Frank Bruno, had his last professional bout in America. It was regrettable that Lewis did not box Riddick Bowe in the paid ranks, as this fight would have been a sure fire-winner with the fans and a possibly epic encounter. It was a fight that was much talked about, but did not come to fruition. Such a contest would have been a chance for Bowe to avenge his amateur defeat and for Lewis to confirm that he was the superior boxer not just in the unpaid ranks, but also in the professional code. Sadly, the fight will have to be listed as the one that got away, leaving fans with their own opinions on who would have won had they clashed in the ring.

Lewis was awarded an MBE and later a CBE. In 2008, he was inducted into the World Boxing Hall of Fame and in 2009, a further honour was bestowed upon him when he was inducted into the International Hall of Fame.

Klitschko may not have got his much hoped-for return with the British fighter, but he did not fare too badly in his career. He twice captured the WBC world heavyweight championship and, with his younger brother, Wladimir, dominated the heavyweight division, turning back a number of challengers during his long reign. Lewis bowed out of the game, having beaten an exceptional fighter in Vitali Klitschko, a fact that will only add to his outstanding legacy in the sport.

APPENDIX I

Boxing Records

Abbreviations

W	Won
WPTS	Won on points
LPTS	Lost on points
WRSF	Won, referee stopped fight
LRSF	Lost, referee stopped fight
WKO	Won by a knockout
LKO	Lost by a knockout
WDQ	Won by a disqualification
LDQ	Lost by a disqualification
WRTD	Won when an opponent retired from the contest
LRTD	Lost when retired from contest
D	Draw

Frank Bruno

No.	Opponent	Result	Date	Location
1	Lupe Guerra	WKO 1	17 March 1982	Kensington
2	Harvey Steichen	WRSF 2	30 March 1982	Wembley
3	Abdul Muhaymin	WKO 1	20 April 1982	Kensington
4	Ronald Gibbs	WRSF 4	4 May 1982	Wembley
5	Tony Moore	WRSF 2	1 June 1982	Kensington
6	George Scott	WRSF 1	14 September 1982	Wembley

7	Ali Lukasa	WRSF 2	23 October 1982	Berlin
8	Rudy Gauwe	WKO 2	9 November 1982	Kensington
9	George Butzbach	WRSF 1	23 November 1982	Wembley
10	Gilberto Acuna	WRSF 1	7 December 1982	Kensington
11	Stewart Lithgo	WRTD 4	18 January 1983	Kensington
12	Peter Mulindwa Kozza	WKO 3	8 February 1983	Kensington
13	Winston Allen	WRSF 2	1 March 1983	Kensington
14	Eddie Neilson	WRSF 3	5 April 1983	Kensington
15	Scott LeDoux	WRSF 3	3 May 1983	Wembley
16	Barry Funches	WRSF 5	31 May 1983	Kensington
17	Mike Jameson	WKO 2	9 July 1983	Chicago
18	Bill Sharkey	WKO 1	27 September 1983	Wembley
19	Floyd Cummings	WRSF 7	11 October 1983	Kensington
20	Walter Santemore	WKO 4	6 December 1983	Kensington
21	Juan Antonio Figueroa	WRSF 1	13 March 1984	Wembley
22	James Smith	LKO 10	13 May 1984	Wembley
23	Ken Lakusta	WKO 2	25 September 1984	Wembley
24	Jeff Jordan	WRSF 3	6 November 1984	Kensington
25	Philipp Brown	WPTS 10	27 November 1984	Wembley
26	Lucien Rodriguez	WRSF 1	26 March 1985	Wembley

European Heavyweight Title

27	Anders Eklund	WKO 4	1 October 1985	Wembley
28	Larry Frazier	WKO 2	4 December 1985	Kensington
29	Gerrie Coetzee	WKO 1	4 March 1986	Wembley

WBA World Heavyweight title

30	Tim Witherspoon	LRSF 11	19 July 1986	Wembley
31	James Tillis	WRSF 5	24 March 1987	Wembley
32	Chuck Gardner	WRSF1	27 June 1987	Cannes
33	Reggie Gross	WRSF 8	30 August 1987	Marbella
34	Joe Bugner	WRSF 8	24 October 1987	Tottenham

WBA, WBC, IBF World Heavyweight Titles

35	Mike Tyson	LRSF 5	25 February 1989	Las Vegas
36	John Emmen	WRSF 1	20 November 1991	Kensington
37	Jose Ribalta	WKO 2	22 April 1992	Wembley
38	Pierre Coetzer	WRSF 8	17 October 1992	Wembley
39	Carl Williams	WRSF 10	24 April 1993	Birmingham

40	Lennox Lewis	LRSF 7	1 October 1993	Cardiff
41	Jesse Ferguson	WRSF 1	16 March 1994	Birmingham
42	Rodolfo Marin	WKO 1	18 February 1995	Shepton Mallet
43	Mike Evans	WKO 2	13 May 1995	Glasgow

WBC World Heavyweight Titles

44	Oliver McCall	WPTS 12	2 September 1995	Wembley
45	Mike Tyson	LRSF 3	16 March 1996	Las Vegas

Lennox Lewis

No.	Opponent	Result	Date	Location
1	Al Malcolm	WCO 2	27 June 1989	Kensington
2	Bruce Johnson	WRSF 2	21 July 1989	Atlantic City
3	Andrew Gerrard	WRSF 4	25 September 1989	Crystal Palace
4	Steve Garber	WKO 1	10 October 1989	Hull
5	Melvin Epps	WDQ 2	5 November 1989	Kensington
6	Greg Gorrell	WRSF 5	18 December 1989	Ontario
7	Noel Quarless	WRSF 2	31 January 1990	Bethnal Green
8	Calvin Jones	WKO 1	22 March 1990	Gateshead
9	Michael Simuwelu	WRSF 1	14 April 1990	Kensington
10	Jorge Alfredo Dascola	WKO 1	9 May 1990	Kensington
11	Dan Murphy	WRSF 6	20 May 1990	Sheffield
12	Ossie Ocasio	WPTS 8	27 June 1990	Kensington
13	Mike Acey	WKO 2	11 July 1990	Ontario

European Heavyweight Title

14	Jean-Maurice Chanet	WRSF 6	31 October 1990	Crystal Palace

British and European Heavyweight Titles

15	Gary Mason	WRSF 7	6 March 1991	Wembley
16	Mike Weaver	WKO 6	12 July 1991	Lake Tahoe

British and European Heavyweight Titles

17	Glen McCrory	WKO 2	30 September 1991	Kensington
18	Tyrell Biggs	WRSF 3	23 November 1991	Atlanta
19	Levi Billups	WPTS 10	1 February 1992	Las Vegas

British, European, and Commonwealth Heavyweight Titles

20	Derek Williams	WRSF 3	30 April 1992	Kensington
21	Mike Dixon	WRSF 4	11 August 1992	Atlantic City

Commonwealth Heavyweight Title and Eliminator for WBC Crown

22	Donovan Ruddock	WRSF 2	31 October 1992	Earls Court

WBC World Heavyweight Title

23	Tony Tucker	WPTS 12	8 May 1993	Las Vegas
24	Frank Bruno	WRSF 7	1 October 1993	Cardiff
25	Phil Jackson	WRSF 8	6 May 1994	Atlantic City
26	Oliver McCall	LRSF 2	24 September 1994	Wembley
27	Lionel Butler	WRSF 5	13 May 1995	Sacramento
28	Justin Fortune	WRSF 4	2 July 1995	Dublin

IBC Heavyweight Title

29	Tommy Morrison	WRSF 6	7 October 1995	Atlantic City
30	Ray Mercer	WPTS 10	10 May 1996	New York

WBC Heavyweight Title

31	Oliver McCall	WRSF 5	7 February 1997	Las Vegas
32	Henry Akinwande	WDQ 5	12 July 1997	Lake Tahoe
33	Andrew Golota	WRSF 1	4 October 1997	Atlantic City
34	Shannon Briggs	WRSF 5	28 March 1998	Atlantic City
35	Željko Mavrović	WPTS 12	26 September 1998	Uncasville

WBC, WBA, IBF Heavyweight Titles

36	Evander Holyfield	D12	13 March 1999	New York

WBC, WBA, IBF, and IBO Heavyweight Titles

37	Evander Holyfield	WPTS 12	13 November 1999	Las Vegas

WBC, IBF, and IBO Heavyweight Titles

38	Michael Grant	WKO 2	29 April 2000	New York
39	Frans Botha	WRSF 2	15 July 2000	Millwall
40	David Tua	WPTS 12	11 November 2000	Las Vegas
41	Hasim Rahman	LKO 5	22 April 2001	Brakpan
42	Hasim Rahman	WKO 4	17 November 2001	Las Vegas
43	Mike Tyson	WKO 8	8 June 2002	Memphis

WBC and IBO Heavyweight Titles

44	Vitali Klitschko	WRSF 6	21 June 2003	Los Angeles

APPENDIX II

Referees Who Officiated at Frank Bruno World Title Fights

Mills Lane (USA)
Frank Bruno *v*. Mike Tyson, 16 March 1996.

Tony Perez (USA)
Frank Bruno *v*. Oliver McCall, 2 September 1995.

Isidro Rodriguez (Venezuela)
Frank Bruno *v*. Tim Witherspoon, 19 July 1986.

Richard Steele (USA)
Frank Bruno *v*. Mike Tyson, 25 February 1989.

Mickey Vann (UK)
Lennox Lewis *v*. Frank Bruno, 1 October 1993.

APPENDIX III

Referees Who Officiated at Lennox Lewis World Title Fights

Frank Cappuccino (USA)
Lennox Lewis *v.* Shannon Briggs, 28 March 1998.
Lennox Lewis *v.* Željko Mavrović, 26 September 1998.

Joe Cortez (USA)
Lennox Lewis *v.* Tony Tucker, 8 May 1993.
Lennox Lewis *v.* Andrew Golota, 4 October 1997.
Lennox Lewis *v.* David Tua, 11 November 2000.
Lennox Lewis *v.* Hasim Rahman, 17 November 2001.

Eddie Cotton (USA)
Lennox Lewis *v.* Mike Tyson, 8 June 2002

Daniel Van de Wiele (Belgium)
Lennox Lewis *v.* Hasim Rahman, 22 April 2001.

José Guadalupe Garcia (Mexico)
Lennox Lewis *v.* Oliver McCall, 24 September 1994.

Mitch Halpern (USA)
Lennox Lewis *v.* Evander Holyfield, 13 November 1999.

Mills Lane (USA)
Lennox Lewis *v.* Oliver McCall, 7 February 1997.
Lennox Lewis *v.* Henry Akinwande, 12 July 1997.

Arthur Mercante Snr (USA)
Lennox Lewis *v.* Phil Jackson, 6 May 1994.

Arthur Mercante Jnr (USA)
Lennox Lewis *v.* Evander Holyfield, 13 March 1999.
Lennox Lewis *v.* Michael Grant, 29 April 2000.

Lou Moret (USA)
Lennox Lewis *v.* Vitali Klitschko, 21 June 2003.

Larry O' Connell (UK)
Lennox Lewis *v.* Frans Botha, 15 July 2000.

Mickey Vann (UK)
Lennox Lewis *v.* Frank Bruno, 1 October 1993.

APPENDIX IV

Judges who officiated at the world title bouts of Frank Bruno

Frank Bruno *v.* Tim Witherspoon, 19 July 1986.
Carlos Sucre (USA); Marcos A. Torres (Panama); Takeshi Shimakawa (Japan).

Frank Bruno *v.* Mike Tyson I, 25 February 1989.
Jerry Roth (USA); Omar Mintun (Mexico); Rodolfo Maldonado (Panama).

Frank Bruno *v.* Lennox Lewis, 1 October 1993.
Tony Castellano (USA); Jerry Roth (USA); Adrian Morgan (UK).

Frank Bruno *v.* Oliver McCall, 2 September 1995.
Ray Solis (Mexico); Newton Campos (Brazil); Malcom Bulner (Australia).

Frank Bruno *v.* Mike Tyson II, 16 March 1996.
Larry O'Connell (UK); Anek Hongtongkam (Thailand); Jerry Roth (USA).

APPENDIX V

Judges Who Officiated at the World Title Bouts of Lennox Lewis

Lennox Lewis *v.* Tony Tucker, 8 May 1993.
Jerry Roth (USA); Harry Gibbs (UK); Mickey Vann (UK).

Lennox Lewis *v.* Frank Bruno, 1 October 1993.
Tony Castellano (USA); Jerry Roth (USA); Adrian Morgan (UK).

Lennox Lewis *v.* Phil Jackson, 6 May 1994.
Bob Logist (Belgium); John Stewart (USA); John Keene (UK).

Lennox Lewis *v.* Oliver McCall I, 24 September 1994.
Franz Marti (Switzerland); Giuseppe Ferrari (Italy); Jae-Bong Kim (South Korea).

Lennox Lewis *v.* Oliver McCall II, 7 February 1997.
Anek Hongtongkam (Thailand); Larry O' Connell (UK); Dalby Shirley (USA).

Lennox Lewis *v.* Henry Akinwande, 12 July 1997.
Terry Smith (USA); Larry O'Connell (UK); Dalby Shirley (USA).

Lennox Lewis *v.* Andrew Golota, 4 October 1997.
Marty Denkin (USA); Chuck Hassett (USA); Barbara Perez (USA).

Lennox Lewis *v.* Shannon Briggs, 28 March 1998.
Anek Hongtongkam (Thailand); Terry O' Connor (UK); John Stewart (USA).

Lennox Lewis *v.* Željko Mavrović, 26 September 1998.
Tom Kaczmarek (USA); Franco Ciminale (Italy); Bob Logist (Belguim).

Lennox Lewis *v.* Evander Holyfield, 13 March 1999.
Stanley Christodoulou (South Africa); Eugenia Williams (USA); Larry O'Connell (UK)

Lennox Lewis *v.* Evander Holyfield, 13 November 1999.
Chuck Giampa (USA); Bill Graham (USA); Jerry Roth (USA).

Lennox Lewis *v.* Michael Grant, 29 April 2000.
Melvina Lathan (USA); Anek Hongtongkam (Thailand); Steve Weisfeld (USA).

Lennox Lewis *v.* Frans Botha, 15 July 2000.
Chuck Williams (USA); Roy Francis (UK); Al Bennett (USA).

Lennox Lewis *v.* David Tua, 11 November 2000.
Jerry Roth (USA); Dave Moretti (USA); Chuck Giampa (USA).

Lennox Lewis *v.* Hasim Rahman, 22 April 2001.
Dave Parris (England); Valerie Dorsett (USA); Thabo Spampool (South Africa).

Lennox Lewis *v.* Hasim Rahman, 17 November 2001.
Patricia Morse Jarman (USA); Dave Moretti (USA); Dalby Shirley (USA).

Lennox Lewis *v.* Mike Tyson, 8 June 2002.
Alfred Buqwana (South Africa); Anek Hongtongkam (Thailand); Bob Logist (Belgium).

Lennox Lewis *v.* Vitali Klitschko, 21 June 2003.
James Jen-Kin (USA); Tom Kaczmarek (USA); Pat Russell (USA).

APPENDIX VI

Pre-Lewis British Heavyweight Challenges

Charlie Mitchell

On 25 January 1894, Charlie Mitchell became the first British boxer to challenge for the world heavyweight crown under the Marquess of Queensberry Rules when he met American holder James J. Corbett at the Duall Athletic Club in Jacksonville, Florida. Mitchell failed to take the championship when knocked out in round three.

Bob Fitzsimmons

Bob Fitzsimmons won the world heavyweight crown on 17 March 1897 by knocking out holder James J. Corbett in round fourteen at the Race Track Arena in Carson City. Fitzsimmons then lost the crown in his first defence to James J. Jeffries on 9 June 1899 at the Athletic Club in Brooklyn, New York, when knocked out in the eleventh round by his American challenger. Fitzsimmons failed to regain the title from Jeffries at The Arena in San Francisco, California on 25 July 1902, when knocked out in round eight.

Gunner Moir

Gunner Moir challenged title holder Tommy Burns of Canada for the world heavyweight title on 2 December 1907 at the National Sport Club at Covent Garden in London. Burns made a successful defence of his crown when he knocked out Moir in round ten. This was the first world heavyweight title fight to take place in the UK.

Jack Palmer

On 10 February 1908, Tommy Burns turned back another UK challenger when he knocked out Jack Palmer in round four at the Wonderland in Whitechapel Road, London.

Jem Roche

Dublin-born Jem Roche failed in his challenge for the world heavyweight crown when knocked out in the opening round on 17 March 1908 at the Theatre Royal Dublin, Ireland. At the time, Ireland was still part of the United Kingdom.

Jewey Smith

On 18 April 1908 at the Neuilly Bowling Palace in Paris, France, Jewey Smith failed to win the world heavyweight crown when champion Tommy Burns retained the title by way of a knockout in round five.

Tommy Farr

Tommy Farr challenged for the world heavyweight crown when he met American holder Joe Louis of the USA at the Yankee Stadium in the Bronx, New York City, on 30 August 1937. He lost a fifteen-round points decision, becoming the first British challenger to go the distance in a world heavyweight title bout.

Bruce Woodcock

On 6 June 1950, Bruce Woodcock failed to win the vacant British & European Boxing Union's version of the world heavyweight crown, when he retired in round four against American Lee Savold in a contest that took place at the White City Stadium, Shepherds Bush, London.

Don Cockell

Don Cockell threw the gauntlet down on 16 May 1955 at the Kezar Stadium, San Francisco, against reigning world heavyweight king Rocky Marciano. The bout concluded in round nine, whereupon Marciano ended the challenge of Cockell by way of a stoppage.

Brian London

On 1 May 1959, Brian London attempted to win the big prize when he entered the ring at the Fairgrounds Coliseum in Indianapolis, Indiana. The defending champion, Floyd Patterson, turned back the challenge of the British fighter by knocking him out in round eleven.

Henry Cooper

Henry Cooper stepped into the ring on 21 May 1966 at the Arsenal Stadium, Highbury, London, in an attempt to wrest the WBC world heavyweight crown away from American holder Muhammad Ali, but failed in his efforts when stopped in round six.

Brian London

Brian London had a second chance to bring the global championship to the UK, but failed in his challenge on 6 August 1966 at the Exhibition Centre in Earls Court, London, when Muhammad Ali retained his WBC world heavyweight crown via a knockout in round three.

Joe Bugner

Joe Bugner next stepped up to the plate on 1 July 1975 at the Merdeka Stadium, Kula Lumpur, Malaysia, in an attempt to take the world heavyweight crown from Muhammad Ali. The title remained in the USA when Ali emerged the victor on points over fifteen rounds.

Richard Dunn

Richard Dunn challenged Muhammad Ali on 25 May 1976 at the Olympiahalle in Munich, Germany, but his hopes of victory ended in round five when the defending champion stopped him in said stanza. Dunn became the first British boxer with the southpaw stance to challenge for this title.

Frank Bruno

On 19 July 1986, Frank Bruno failed to win the WBA version of the world heavyweight title when American holder Tim Witherspoon stopped him in round eleven at Wembley Stadium in London.

Frank Bruno

Frank Bruno stepped into the ring at the Hilton Hotel in Las Vegas, USA, on 25 February 1989 to challenge American holder Mike Tyson for the undisputed world heavyweight crown. The Briton's bid came to an end in round five when the referee stopped the contest in the champion's favour.